# SAND TABLE EXERCISES

BY

## CAPTAIN A. W. VALENTINE, M.B.E.

*The Devonshire Regiment*

WITH A FOREWORD BY

## COLONEL E. HEWLETT, C.M.G., D.S.O., O.B.E., *p.s.c.*

*General Staff*

*Comprising 10 Sand Table Exercises suitable for N.C.Os. of the Regular Army and Territorial Army and for Cadets of Officers' Training Corps.*

*With 8 Maps, over 50 Sand Table Problems and Solutions, and 20 Questions and Answers suitable for N.C.Os.' Promotion Examinations.*

## The Naval & Military Press Ltd

*Published by*

## The Naval & Military Press Ltd

Unit 5 Riverside, Brambleside
Bellbrook Industrial Estate
Uckfield, East Sussex
TN22 1QQ England

Tel: +44 (0)1825 749494

www.naval-military-press.com
www.nmarchive.com

# FOREWORD

A SAND table, on which a piece of ground can be modelled, and thereby bring the country, so to speak, indoors, is unquestionably essential for tactical instruction.

For those, and there are many, who can seldom get out on to the ground itself, the indoor model provides a valuable substitute for the real thing ; whilst for those who are fortunate enough to have suitable ground available, the model on the sand table will be found to provide a useful auxiliary.

But, although exercises on the sand table have for some time been recognized as a valuable means of teaching minor tactics, it is still the exception rather than the rule to find useful instruction being given by this method. The reason for this is fairly obvious. Some of us have little or no idea how to set about it, whilst others lack the imagination or time, both of which are required in order to produce really useful exercises.

In this Book, " Sand Table Exercises," Captain Valentine tells us how to prepare our model of the ground, and gives us a series of most useful and carefully considered exercises for junior N.C.Os., the result of much personal experience of this form of instruction.

The exercises deal in turn with the various tactical phases in which the student is likely to find himself placed—e.g., attack, defence, protection, withdrawal—and in each of these phases a series of concrete problems is introduced requiring definite decisions by the student as a platoon or section commander. A well-considered solution is given to each of these problems.

The following points in the preparation of the models should be stressed. If possible, get the N.C.Os. themselves to prepare the models from the maps. It arouses their interest, and at the same time provides most useful training in map-reading. Avoid using the same model too often. The great value of the sand table is that you can change your ground at will.

This Book will be found most useful to anyone engaged in teaching minor tactics, and more especially to those who, for one reason or another, have not been able to think out exercises for themselves.

E. HEWLETT, Colonel,<br>General Staff.

Aldershot,
*October*, 1931.

# CONTENTS

# INTRODUCTION

THIS book consists of ten simple Sand Table Exercises for use in instructing N.C.Os. in section leading.

Each exercise consists of—

A. Notes for a lecture on the subject of the exercise. These notes are intended to be read in conjunction with " Infantry Training," Vol. II, Infantry Section Leading, and " Small Arms Training."
B. A narrative.
C. Problems and notes for solutions.
D. A plan of the sand table model to be used for the exercise.

It is suggested that the exercises be conducted in the following manner :—

(1) Study sand table, pointing out names of places, north point and scale, etc.
(2) Read out the narrative and explain it to the class.
(3) Take each problem in turn and all class consider it.
(4) Having given them time to consider the problem, call on N.C.Os. in turn to give their solutions.

In cases where orders have to be given, the N.C.O. called on for a solution should actually give his orders to the remainder of the class as if they represented his section commanders or men of his section, according to the nature of the problem.

Sections should be represented on the sand table and moved by the N.C.Os. as the exercise proceeds.

## THE CONSTRUCTION OF SAND TABLES.

Sand table models should be bright, attractive and realistic, but not elaborate. They should be capable of alteration to another model in at least an hour. N.C.Os. soon become interested in their construction, and a model from one of these plans has often been made for me by two N.C.Os. in half an hour.

Avoid using the same model too often. The class soon become tired of it. For this reason eight models are given in this book, though most of the exercises could quite well be done on one model.

The materials required for the construction of sand tables are—

(1) A tray approximately 6 ft. by 3 ft. 6 in., with sides about 6 in. high. This can be placed on a barrack-room table or across two forms.

(2) Sufficient sand to fill the tray about two-thirds full.

(3) Model houses and sheds. They can easily be made from small blocks of wood and painted attractive colours.

(4) Model trees, bushes, etc., made with wire and green wool.

(5) Strips of loofah, coloured green and brown, to represent hedges.

(6) A quantity of coloured sawdust. Sawdust can easily be dyed any colour by placing it in a sandbag and immersing it in a bucket of dye.

The models should be constructed in the following manner :—

(1) Mould the sand to represent the conformation of the ground according to the form lines given on the plan. It will be noticed that the form lines are numbered 1, 2, 3, etc., to show the lie of the ground.

(2) Place in roads and tracks with sawdust, light coloured powder, or coloured tapes.

(3) Add fields and colour. It will be noticed that the plans are marked CORN, GRASS, etc.

Colour with sawdust as follows :—

| | |
|---|---|
| Corn ... | Natural colour of sawdust. |
| Grass ... | Green. |
| Ploughed | Dark brown. |
| Heath ... | A mixture of brown and green. |

(4) Add villages and complete the remainder of the detail.

(5) Divide up the side of the sand table with chalk marks representing divisions of 100 yards according to the scale. This will be found a great help in estimating distances.

(6) Write the names of the various places on slips of paper and place on the sand table.

Models constructed according to these plans will have rather a bare appearance when completed, and further detail may be added as required.

# SAND TABLE EXERCISES

## SAND TABLE EXERCISE No. 1
### THE USE OF GROUND—A SECTION STALK
(Model used : Sand Table No. 1)

**1. Object of Exercise.**

The object of this exercise is to train the section commander in the use of ground and formations.

**2. Introductory.**

We read in " Infantry Training," Vol. II, Sec. 13, para. 8, that the " aims of the platoon and section commander should be—

" To advance as close as possible to the enemy position without undue loss and without having to check the speed of the attack by opening fire."

To put this into effect is no easy matter, and in order to do this the section commander must be trained to—

(1) **Select the best line of advance.**
(2) **Maintain his direction.**
(3) **Adopt the formation which best conforms to the ground over which he is moving.**

(1) This should be done methodically and in the following manner :—

(a) First select the position of observation from where line can be observed.
(b) Select position from where he is going to fire.
(c) Which line gives him the best covered approach.
(d) What obstacles are in his way.
(e) Protection.

(2) This is best done by picking out prominent objects as landmarks on the line of advance. The section commander must remember that all men in his section must know the direction of the advance, otherwise they may lose direction if he becomes a casualty.

(3) This is best learnt by actual practice on the ground. The section commander should be guided by the fact that the close

1

formations such as file and single file conform better to the ground and are easy to control, but do not give such good fire effect or protection as the open formations such as arrowhead and line.

### 3. Exercise No. 1.

A. NARRATIVE

An enemy patrol has been located at WHITE FARM. You are O.C. No. 3 Section, and you are in position just in rear of GREEN WOOD.

B. PROBLEM.

By the use of ground, to lead your section so close to the enemy patrol that you can shoot with a certainty of killing them.

C. METHOD OF CONDUCTING THE EXERCISE.

(1) Having given out the narrative and the problems to the whole class, show them No. 3 Section, which you have placed in the position marked X.

(2) All students consider problem from point of view of O.C. No. 3 Section.

(3) Having given them a few minutes to consider this problem, ask them in turn the following questions :—

Q. 1. How near do you think that you would want to get to an enemy section to shoot with a certainty of killing them ?

Q. 2. What position would you select to observe your line from ?

Q. 3. What position would you choose as your final fire position, and why ?

Q. 4. Which line gives you the best covered approach ?

Q. 5. What obstacles are in your way ?

Q. 6. Move your section on the sand table along the line of advance you have selected.

NOTES FOR SOLUTION.

A. 1. Not more than 100 yards away, and nearer if possible. Bring out the point that, whereas on the range under ideal contions they may all be able to shoot accurately up to 500 yards, it is a very different matter when—

(a) They have just done a possibly fatiguing movement.

(b) They are naturally excited.

A. 2. The high ground at X.

A 3. The hedge at Y, because it is near the objective, appears to be a good position, and has the best line of approach to it.

*A*. 4. A suggested line is shown on the map by means of a dotted line. This line makes the most use of natural cover.

*A*. 5. The only obstacles in this case are the open spaces between the cover which must be crossed.

*A*. 6. This will bring out the use of the various formations. The section commander must be made to split his advance up into " bounds," and say what formation he would adopt for the various " bounds."

# SAND TABLE MODEL No. 1

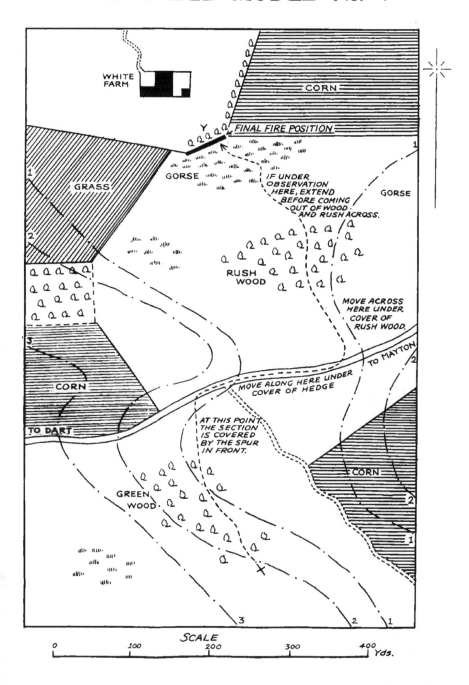

# SAND TABLE EXERCISE No. 2

## FIRE ORDERS

(Model used : Sand Table No. 2)

### 1. Object of the Exercise.

To practise a section commander in indicating targets and controlling fire

### 2. Introduction.

Section commanders are practised in fire orders on landscape targets, miniature and 30 yards ranges, and in the open, but seldom on sand tables. Undoubtedly the best form of practice is in the open, but this is not always possible for a variety of reasons. Weather conditions, the position of barracks or drill halls, and the time at which classes have to be held are various factors which influence this.

When instructions in fire orders have to be given indoors, they can be carried out very satisfactorily on the sand table. An actual situation can be given, and the section commanders can consider how they would apply and control their fire.

### 3. Exercise No. 2.

A. NARRATIVE.

At point *X* (show on sand table) there is a defended post occupied by a Lewis gun section. This is part of a locality held by a platoon.

B. PROBLEMS.

**(1) Situation 1.**—You are N.C.O. i/c of this Lewis gun section.
**Problem 1.**—Select reference points on your front and point them out to your section.
**Notes for Solution, Problem 1.**—Suggested reference points— KNOWLE FARM, EXE WOOD.
Reference points should be given out in the following manner :—
" You all see that farm about 300 yards away on the right of the road. That will be a reference point. Call that FARM. The range to that is 300 yards."
Similarly EXE WOOD would probably be described, and the nearest corner indicated. This might be called WOOD.
The following situations and problems could then be taken, each problem being discussed before proceeding to the next situation.

5

**(2) Situation 2.**—The post has been occupied since dawn. It is now 1400 hours and there are no covering troops in front. Two enemy scouts are seen on the road BLACKTOWN—EXHAM, at the point where the road appears from the rear of LONG WOOD marked (*A*).

**Problem 2.**—What action would you take ?

**Notes for Solution, Problem 2.**—This is a situation where an **anticipatory fire order** may be given.

EXAMPLE.—" No. 4 Section—400—Point where road appears from behind wood—5 bursts rapid—Await my order to fire."

*Or*

" No. 4 Section—400—Farm left 11 o'clock—Point where road appears—5 bursts rapid—Await my order to fire."

**(3) Situation 3.**—A section appears and is engaged by you. They are seen to double across from the road into SMALL WOOD. Shortly after this you see an enemy section getting into position on the forward edge of this wood.

**Problem 3.**—Get the fire of your Lewis gun on to this section.

**Notes for Solution, Problem 3.**—A **normal** fire order may be given in this situation.

EXAMPLE.—" No. 4 Section—350—Last target—Slightly left, small wood—At near end—5 bursts—FIRE."

**(4) Situation 4.**—The next thing that you observe is that an enemy section appears from LONG WOOD and rushes in extended line to the track which runs from KNOWLE FARM to the road. To the naked eye they appear to have good cover, but you see through your glasses that they present a good target.

**Problem 4.**—What fire order would you give ?

**Notes for Solution, Problem 4.**—A **normal** fire order may be given in this situation, introducing the method of distributing fire along a hedge.

EXAMPLE.—" No. 4 Section—Gun and rifles—300—Farm— Left 9 o'clock—Along hedgerow between Farm and road— 5 bursts—FIRE."

The points to note here are that each rifleman should select a point on the hedgerow according to his position in the section, and should fire at this point. The target is thus distributed amongst the section. The Lewis gun should distribute in bursts along the target.

**(5) Situation 5.**—Some enemy movement is next seen on the left of WYE HILL. A section appears and rushes across the road at *B*. This is engaged by another section of your platoon on your left. A few minutes later another enemy section appears from KNOWLE FARM, and starts to advance across the open in extended order.

**Problem 5.**—What fire order would you give ?

**Notes for Solution, Problem 5.**—A **normal** fire order to catch the enemy in the open.

EXAMPLE.—" No. 4 Section—Gun and rifles—250—Slightly right—Enemy section advancing 5 rounds—FIRE."

(6) **Situation 6.**—Two smoke grenades burst just upwind of your post. As the smoke clears you see an enemy section is rushing you from the direction of the road at *C*.

**Problem 6.**—What would you do ?

**Notes for Solution, Problem 6.**—This is the sort of situation where a brief fire order is necessary.

EXAMPLE.—" Gun and Rifles, sights down—Quarter right— enemy advancing—RAPID FIRE."

NOTE.—A fire control order given to a Lewis gun section infers that the gun only will fire unless—

(a) Gun and rifles are required, when the order will be preceded by " **Gun and rifles.**"

(b) Riflemen only are required, when the order will be preceded by " **Riflemen only.**"

# SAND TABLE MODEL No. 2

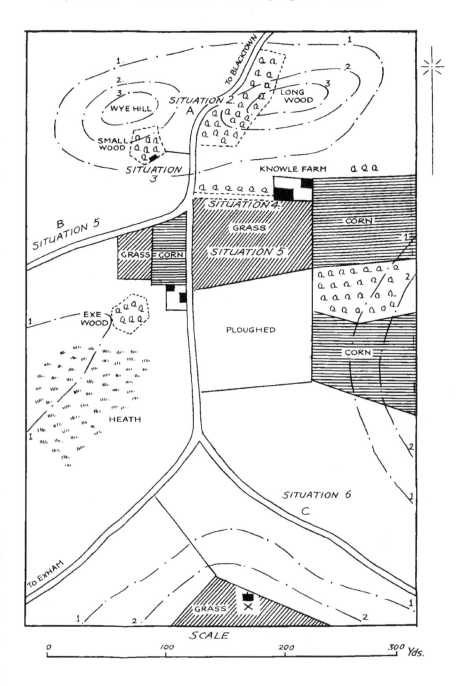

SCALE

0            100            200            300 Yds.

# SAND TABLE EXERCISE No. 3.

## PATROLS

(Model used : Sand Table No. 3)

### 1. Object of the Exercise.

To train section commanders in patrol leading.

### 2. Introductory.

(1) **Reconnoitring Patrols.**—These are constantly sent out by the forward companies in outposts and defence, during the hours of darkness and always before dawn. Their duty is to avoid contact with the enemy, and to gain information without fighting. STRENGTH.—Usually a complete section. It is sometimes taught that a reconnoitring patrol should be composed of a few selected men, but this does not work well in practice. Selected men will find themselves constantly employed on this duty, whilst the others are escaping it.

(2) **Fighting Patrols.**—A fighting patrol has the same duty— *i.e.*, to gain information—but it is made sufficiently strong to dominate any hostile patrols, and to capture prisoners. STRENGTH.—Usually a complete platoon, commanded by an officer.

(3) **Orders to a Patrol.**—" **The success of a patrol depends principally on the leader. It is essential that he should be given clear and definite orders.**" (" Infantry Training," Vol. II, 1931, Sec. 24, para. 7.)

The patrol leader should be given orders on the following points :—

(a) What is known of the enemy dispositions, and the points on which he is required to bring back information. **Definite questions will produce definite answers.**

(b) Approximate route that he is to follow, how far he is to go, and how long he is to be out.

(c) The probable movement of other friendly troops in the neighbourhood.

(d) The password.

(4) **Formation.**—DAY.—In very open country a section might move in arrowhead, and a platoon in diamond. In close country or cultivation it is best to move the patrol by " bounds " in the following manner.

B                                                        9

Divide the section into three pairs. Select some spot a convenient distance ahead, and send the first pair forward to this. If they signal all clear they can move forward to the next " bound," and the second pair may move up to the position that they have just left. Similarly, the last pair can move forward to the first " bound " when the first pair are moving to the third.

The patrol would then be situated like this :—

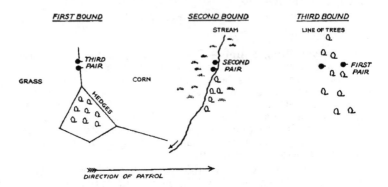

If a patrol is moved in this manner there is little chance of it being surprised, and even if attacked by a superior force, one pair at least will probably be able to return with information.

A fighting patrol of a platoon could be moved in the same manner, using sections instead of pairs.

NIGHT.—The formation should not be too wide so as to lose touch, nor should it be too close so as to risk ambush. A formation such as the above, only very much closed up, would probably be suitable.

(5) **Dress.**—Equipment light ; a bandolier is often all that is necessary. No grenades ; a nervous man might throw one and endanger the patrol. No distinctive badges, buttons or papers. All men warned that they are not to give away any information.

### 3. Exercise No. 3.

A. NARRATIVE.

You are O.C. No. 15 Section of a platoon in the defended locality pointed out to you on the sand table. The position has been prepared for defence, and there are now no covering troops in front. At dawn this morning three enemy were seen retiring from WHITE FARM, which is in a ruined state.

**Notes for conducting the Exercise.**—In this exercise the position of every man should be studied. For this purpose use " Halma " men or some other substitute to represent the men of the section on the sand table.

All should consider the following problems, and then N.C.Os. may be selected to give their solutions and actually move the men in the sand table.

B. PROBLEMS.

**(1) Situation 1.**—At about 1930 hours your platoon commander sends for you and gives you the following orders :—

" I want you to take your section out on a reconnoitring patrol. The only enemy we have seen are the three men who retired from WHITE FARM early this morning. I expect they lie up there by night. **I want to know if there are any enemy in WHITE FARM and PINE WOOD.**

" You will proceed along the road to UPTON as far as WHITE FARM, thence to PINE WOOD, returning across country to No. 16 Section's post. You will go out at 2359 hours and return at 0100 hours. The password is ' Nightmare.' Any questions ?"

**Problem 1.**—It will be dark in one hour. What preparations would you make for this patrol ?

**Notes for Solution, Problem 1.**—(*a*) Explain the orders to your section so that should you become a casualty they will know what to do.

(*b*) Have a good look at the ground with your section and point out where you are going and notice any landmarks which will help you to find your way in the dark. As far as PINE WOOD this presents no difficulty, as you can more or less follow the road.

After leaving PINE WOOD you have to come across country, and you should notice the positions of various woods, which will be a guide to you on your return. On a moonlight night the small clump of trees on the left of No. 13 Section's post would probably be helpful, as being on the skyline it would show up from some distance.

A platoon commander sometimes arranges to send up a light signal if a patrol does not return when it is expected, in order to guide them if they have lost their way.

(*c*) Warn the men that no papers or badges will be taken, and tell them that should they be captured they are on no account to give away any information.

(*d*) Give orders about dress and equipment, as follows :—

(i) No equipment will be taken.
(ii) Bayonets will be fixed.
(iii) Magazines will be charged.

B 2

(iv) Twenty-five rounds per man will be taken in a bandolier.

(v) No grenades.

(2) **Situation 2.**—You move off with your patrol at 2359 hours.

**Problem 2.**—How would you move your patrol up to WHITE FARM ? and on arrival there what steps would you take to find out if it is occupied ?

**Notes for Solution, Problem 2.**—In considering this problem the students should actually move the patrol along the sand table to show the formation which should be similar to that described in para. 2 (4), with the men on either side of the road.

In order to find out if the farm is occupied, it should be approached carefully and with as little noise as possible. The section commander should dispose his men so that, if he is rushed, at least one man can escape. He should then send one pair forward to listen near the farm for movement. Sooner or later, if the farm is occupied, he will hear something.

The position of the patrol would then be something like this :—

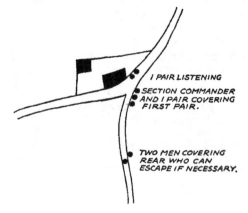

I PAIR LISTENING

SECTION COMMANDER AND I PAIR COVERING FIRST PAIR.

TWO MEN COVERING REAR WHO CAN ESCAPE IF NECESSARY.

If the forward pair report that they hear anything, the section commander should himself work his way up as near as possible to the farm so that he can make some estimate of the enemy's strength.

(3) **Situation 3.**—From your observations it appears that the farm is occupied by an enemy cavalry patrol. You see six horses tied up in rear of the farm, and a sentry on the road in front.

**Problem 3.**—What would you do ?

**Notes for Solution, Problem 3.**—There are two courses open to the section commander in this situation—

(*a*) To proceed with his patrol to PINE WOOD and report when he returns to his position that WHITE FARM is occupied.

(*b*) To send back a message reporting the occupation of WHITE FARM, before proceeding to PINE WOOD.

In considering which course to take, the section commander should ask himself, " **Why was I sent out ?**"

To find out if WHITE FARM and PINE WOOD are occupied by the enemy. " **I have found out that WHITE FARM is occupied by a patrol, therefore I should let my platoon commander know, as he may wish to send out a fighting patrol to capture it.**"

The proper course to take in this case would be therefore to send one man back with a message, and then proceed with the patrol.

SUGGESTED MESSAGE.

*To :* 4 Pl.

.........................................................................................................................

*From :* 16 Sec.

.........................................................................................................................

| *Originator's No. :* S.1. | *Date :* 24 | | *In reply to No. :* | |
|---|---|---|---|---|
| WHITE | FARM | occupied | by | patrol |
| enemy | Cavalry | AAA | Sentry | on |
| road | in | front | AAA | Am |
| proceeding | with | patrol. | | |

*Time of origin :* 0030 hrs.          I. Bungle, L/c.

**(4) Situation 4.**—Having dealt with the previous situation, your patrol is now in the vicinity of PINE WOOD. One of your men comes to you and says he has found a disabled enemy trooper lying in the wood. You investigate this, and find that the man has apparently a broken leg. He tells you that he was out with a patrol and lost his way ; his horse got startled in the wood and suddenly bolted, throwing him against a tree.

**Problem 4.**—What would you do ?

**Notes for Solution, Problem 4.**—Prisoners are always important, as useful information can often be obtained from them. You are about half a mile from your position and you have five men, so it would not be an impossible task to improvise some sort of stretcher and carry this man in.

You should, however, remove all badges, buttons and papers from him, which may give you the identity of his regiment, or other information

(5) **Situation 5.**—You are returning with your patrol, and whilst crossing the fields between the two woods marked *A* and *B* (point out on sand table), you hear some movement in the wood on your right.

**Problem 5.**—What action would you take ?

**Notes for Solution, Problem 5.**—A reconnoitring patrol is sent out to gain information and avoid contact with the enemy ; there are cases, however, when a patrol returning might meet a small party of the enemy and not be able to avoid contact. In such cases a determined rush with the bayonet is most effective.

In this situation, however, you have a prisoner and useful information, you have done your job and want to get back. You should therefore try to avoid contact with this party of the enemy and get your prisoner back. Some steps must be taken to prevent him attracting their attention.

(6) **Situation 6.**—You take your patrol back through No. 16 Section's post, and report to your platoon sergeant, who says :—
" The platoon commander has just been called back to Company Headquarters for orders, and he wants a report from you sent down to him."

**Problem 6.**—Write out the report you would render.

**Notes for Solution, Problem 6.**

Patrol Report by L/C. I. Bungle.

O.C. No. 16 Section.

Ref. Ord. Service Sheet 303.

I left the line at 2359 hrs. and proceeded along the road DOWNTOWN—UPTON to vicinity of WHITE FARM. I found WHITE FARM occupied by a patrol of enemy cavalry. I counted six horses tied up in rear of the farm and a sentry on road in front. I reported this and, making a detour, proceeded to PINE WOOD. I found there one enemy trooper who had become detached from his patrol and had his leg broken by being thrown from his horse. Whilst returning I heard movement in the small wood (Map Reference). I did not investigate this.

The regimental badge and two letters found on the prisoner are forwarded with this report.

I. Bungle, L/c.,

O.C. No. 16 Sec.

24th Mar. 30.

# SAND TABLE MODEL No. 3

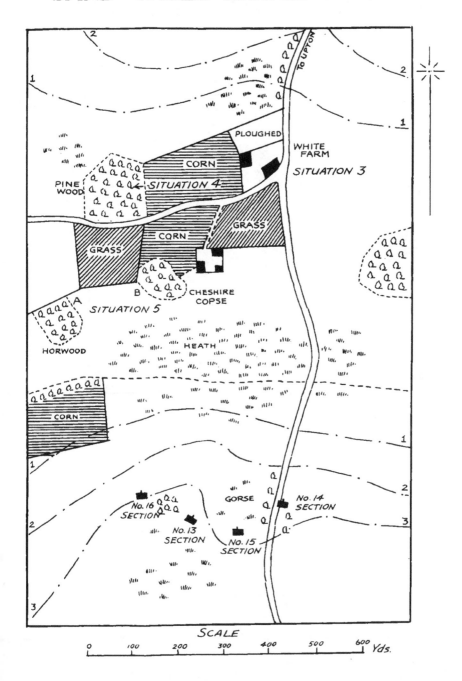

SCALE

0    100    200    300    400    500    600 Yds.

# SAND TABLE EXERCISE No. 4

## THE PLATOON AND SECTION IN THE ATTACK

(Model used : Sand Table No. 4.)

### 1. Object of the Exercise.

To study the actions of platoon and section commanders in various phases of the attack.

### 2. Introductory.

(1) It must be remembered that the platoon is the unit on which all infantry tactics are based, because it is the smallest unit which can be divided up into interdependent units capable of fire and movement. These interdependent bodies are the sections. (" Infantry Training," Vol. II, Sec. 13, para. 1.)

(2) The platoon commander receives his orders from his company commander and is given the task which he is to carry out in the attack—generally to secure a certain objective or make good a certain line. **He must always be quite clear which his objective is on the ground.** He will rarely be employed on a frontage of more than 200 yards.

(3) He returns to his platoon, makes his reconnaissance, and decides on how he will employ his sections, bearing in mind the assistance he may expect to get from artillery, machine guns, etc.

(4) Having examined the ground, he decides how many forward sections it will be necessary to employ. He can adopt any of the formations given below, but there is no hard-and-fast rule that any of these formations should be adopted. The method in which he moves his platoon will depend entirely on the situation, the nature of the ground, and the strength of the enemy.

(5) **Formations**—(a) ONE SECTION FORWARD.—

    (i) Ground is open.
    (ii) Enemy weak.
    (iii) Little is known of enemy strength.

Such is the formation adopted by a vanguard platoon.

15

DIAGRAM 1.

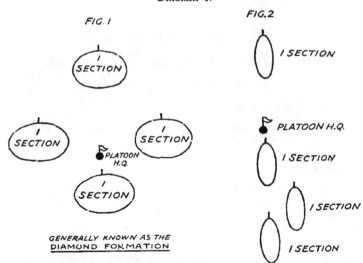

GENERALLY KNOWN AS THE
DIAMOND FORMATION

(b) TWO SECTIONS FORWARD.—When platoon front is wide. Care should be taken that the sections in rear are not placed directly behind the forward sections.

DIAGRAM 2.

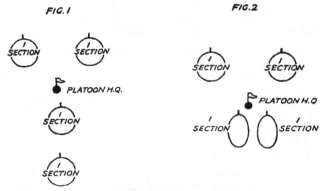

(c) THREE SECTIONS FORWARD.—
    (i) When front is wide.
    (ii) When country is close.

This formation restricts the platoon commander's powers of manœuvre.

DIAGRAM 3.

(6) The section commander receives his orders from the platoon commander and makes arrangements for carrying them out. In practice, it will be found that he has little time in which to do this, if a steady rate of forward movement is to be maintained. He should therefore be trained to make up his mind and act quickly.

He should—

(a) Make sure he knows his objective.
(b) Decide how he is going to get there.
(c) Pick out intermediate positions from where he can bring fire on the enemy. He can then advance by " bounds " from one position to the next.
(d) Decide on formation he is going to adopt.
(e) Maintain fire discipline.

## 3. Exercise No. 4.

A. NARRATIVE.

No. 1 Platoon, 1st Blankshires, is the leading detachment of a vanguard proceeding along the road EASTON—WESTON. Contact with the enemy, who have proceeded in the direction of WESTON, has been lost. There are no cavalry in front, as they have been detached on a special mission.

At 0900 hours to-day No. 1 Section, the leading section of the vanguard, have reached point *A*.

B. PROBLEMS.

(1) **Situation 1.**—The vanguard consists of " A " Company, 1st Blankshires, 1 platoon " D " M.G. Company, 1 section 16th Battery Light Artillery.

**Problem 1.**—(*a*) Given the position of the leading section, where would you expect to find the remaining units of the vanguard ?

(*b*) Show on the sand table the formation in which you would expect to find the leading section of the vanguard.

(*c*) In what formation would you expect to find the remainder of the platoon ?

**Notes for Solution, Problem 1.**—(*a*) The vanguard would probably be disposed on the road as shown in this sketch :—

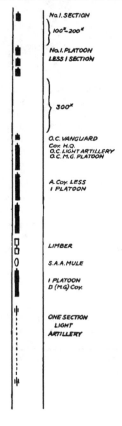

No 1. SECTION

100ˣ-200ˣ

No. 1. PLATOON
LESS 1 SECTION

300ˣ

O.C. VANGUARD
Coy. H.Q.
O.C. LIGHT ARTILLERY
O.C. M.G. PLATOON

A. Coy. LESS
1 PLATOON

LIMBER

S.A.A. MULE

1 PLATOON
D (M.G.) Coy.

ONE SECTION
LIGHT
ARTILLERY

(*b*) This section is the leading section of the vanguard, and he must adopt a formation which will prevent him being surprised. He should have two scouts from 50 to 100 yards ahead of the section, and a suitable formation for the rest of the section would be open file. The men walking on either side of the road, ready to take cover in the hedges if necessary.

NOTE.—**Rifles should be at the trail.**

(*c*) The remaining three sections of the platoon have to be ready for action at any moment. They should therefore be in such a formation that the platoon commander is able to manœuvre them quickly to either flank, if his forward section suddenly gains contact with the enemy.

In order to do this, a formation in which there are intervals between the sections would appear to be most suitable. This gives the platoon commander much more chance of manœuvre, and prevents the possibility of the platoon being pinned to the ground by enemy machine guns, which might happen if the platoon was more concentrated.

A suitable formation is shown in this sketch :—

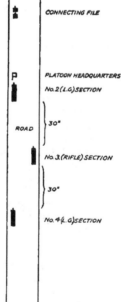

The sections shown are in file.

(2) **Situation 2.**—On reaching point $A$, No. 1 Section is fired on by a light automatic from the hedge at $X$, and one of the scouts is shot through the head. The remainder of the section take cover in the hedge. Any further forward movement brings fire on to your section.

**Problem 2.**—As O.C. No. 1 Section, what action would you take ?

**Notes for Solution, Problem 2.**—Section commanders of forward sections must realize that whenever they are held up they are delaying the whole of the vanguard. In this situation he is unable to move forward without some assistance.

It is therefore his duty to return the fire of the enemy and to let the platoon commander know at once—

(*a*) Where he is held up.

(*b*) What is holding him up.

He should at once send back a verbal message to this effect to his platoon commander :—

> *From: No.* 1 *Sec.*
> *To:* 1 *Pl.*

*Am held up on road about* 200 *yards west of cross roads by enemy light automatic firing from line of trees in front of the GRANGE.*

As soon as he gets an opportunity he should collect the ammunition from the man who has become a casualty.

(3) **Situation 3.**—The remainder of the platoon has not yet come under fire, and is at present in the position shown (marked $B$).

The platoon commander receives a message giving him the information given in Situation 2.

**Problem 3.**—(*a*) As O.C. No. 1 Platoon, what action would you take on receipt of this message ?

(*b*) Give the orders you would issue to your section commanders.

**Notes for Solution, Problem 3.**—(*a*) It is the duty of the platoon commander to act vigorously to overcome this slight resistance, so that he will not delay the advance of the troops behind him.

He should therefore decide at once to attack this enemy post with the remainder of the platoon and drive them out.

(*b*) In order to issue his orders, the section commanders should be called up to the hedge at $Y$, where they can observe the enemy post without being seen.

A point to impress on section commanders here is that when called up by the platoon commander to receive orders, they should never collect in a bunch and thus provide a target for the enemy fire. They should space themselves out as much as possible as long as they are able to hear the platoon commander's orders.

Situations may arise where it will only be possible to bring up section commanders one at a time to view the enemy's position. The following is a suggested way of dealing with this situation.

VERBAL ORDERS BY NO. 1 PLATOON COMMANDER.

1. *Information.*

   *(a) Enemy.* — An enemy post is holding us up from the hedge at *X*. (Indicate the position on the ground.)

   *(b) Own Troops.* — No. 1 Section is held up on the road at a point about 200 yards from here. They are unable to advance farther up the road.

2. *Intention.* — I intend to drive the enemy out of that position.

3. *Method.* — No. 2 Section will move under cover to the spur at LONE TREE HILL and get into position to give covering fire.

I will move with Nos. 3 and 4 Sections under cover along road to the corner of the nearest Cornfield (Point *C*). Thence along hedge to rear of OAK WOOD (Point *D*).

No. 2 Section will then cover movement of No. 4 Section to OAK WOOD, and No. 3 Section to far side of grass field (shown on map).

All then cover advance of No. 1 Section up to far side of grass field.

L.Gs. will then give covering fire whilst Nos. 1 and 3 assault the post. *Move in five minutes' time.*

4. *Intercommunication.* — Platoon H.Q. will move with No. 3 Section.

**(4) Situation 4.**—The section commanders having received the orders of the platoon commanders, go back to their sections and in turn give out their orders.

**Problem 4.**—You are O.C. No. 2 L.G. Section. How would you carry out the task allotted to you ?

**Notes for Solution, Problem 4.**—He has been told to move in 5 minutes' time. He should therefore, in this period, let his section know what he is going to do and how he proposes to do it.

He should give out very brief orders as follows :—

### Orders of No. 2 Section Commander.

1. *Information.*    The enemy are holding us up from that line of trees on left of road about 500 yards from here. No. 1 Section is held up on road about 200 yards ahead of us. Nos. 3 and 4 Sections are advancing on left of road.

2. *Intention.*    I am going to get on to LONE TREE HILL to bring L.G. fire on to the enemy post.

3. *Method.*    Move as follows:—

   1*st Bound :* Along road under cover into HOLM WOOD.

   2*nd Bound :* Under cover of Spur to rear of LONE TREE HILL.

   3*rd Bound :* To a position I will select on LONE TREE HILL.

   I shall then cover any movement I see on left of road.

(5) **Situation 5.**—Nos. 3 and 4 Sections have reached the far edge of the grass field. On No. 2 Section opening fire, five enemy with light automatic were seen to double back from the position at *X*. Two were hit by the fire of No. 2 Section, and the other three were seen to double into the GRANGE.

The position of the four sections of the platoon are now as shown on the sand table (shown in black on the map).

The platoon commander decides to attack and drive the enemy out of the house.

**Problem 5.**—As O.C. No. 1 Platoon, what orders would you issue to carry out the attack on this house ?

**Notes for Solution, Problem 5.**—In this situation it will be possible for him to give out his orders to Nos. 1, 3 and 4 Section commanders as he can signal to them to crawl along the hedge to him.

The problem of communicating with No. 2 Section presents some difficulty, as he is more isolated and should he signal for this signal commander it would probably result in loss of time, with the possibility of the section commander becoming a casualty on his way to receive orders.

**However, if he is well trained, he can rely on him covering any movement he may see.**

The platoon commander would then issue orders similar to the following :—

### Orders of No. 1 Platoon Commander.

| | |
|---|---|
| 1. *Information.* | The enemy are holding the GRANGE. |
| 2. *Intention.* | I intend to attack and drive them out. |
| 3. *Method.* | Nos. 1 and 3 Sections cover by fire the movement of No. 4 Section into HIGH WOOD. Nos. 1 and 3 Sections will then advance to line of trees at $X$. |
| | On getting into position No. 3 Section will fire four smoke grenades in bursts of two to screen the attackers from the GRANGE. |
| | On the bursting of the second pair of grenades Nos. 1 and 3 Sections will assault the house. |
| | Move as soon as you get back to your sections. |
| 4. *Intercommunication.* | Platoon H.Q. will be with No. 3 Section. |

(6) **Situation 6.**—The orders are issued and the section commanders crawl back to their sections.

**Problem 6.**—As O.C. No. 3 Section, having been told to fire four smoke grenades to screen the assault from the house—

    (a) How many smoke grenades have you got in your section ?

    (b) There is a slight wind blowing from left to right. Where would you aim at putting your grenades, and how long do you think the cloud would last ?

**Notes for Solution, Problem 6.**—(a) Nine.

(b) On the left of the house so that the smoke will blow across it. The smoke of one grenade will last for thirty seconds. A screen put up by four grenades could not be relied upon for more than one minute.

**Problem 7.**—As O.C. No. 1 Section, what orders would you give your section ?

**Notes for Solution, Problem 7.**—The orders in this case must be as brief as possible in order to save time.

### Orders of No. 1 Section Commander.

The enemy are holding that large house in front. We are going to give covering fire for No. 4 Section to get into HIGH WOOD. Then we are going to double across to that next hedge, from where we will assault, covered by smoke from No. 3 Section.

(7) **Situation 7.**—The attack is successful. The house is captured, and you find that it was held by a large section of the enemy, all of whom are either casualties or prisoners.

You find that you have 50 per cent. casualties.

**Problem 8.**—As O.C. No. 1 Platoon, what would you do ?

**Notes for Solution, Problem 8.**—The enemy resistance has been overcome, but a platoon after such an attack is not fit to resume its duty as leading detachment of the vanguard.

The platoon commander should at once reorganize his platoon, taking up a position in front of the house with one section on the road so as to be prepared against a counter-attack.

The company commander must be informed of the progress of this section so that he can detail another platoon to take over the duties of leading detachment of the vanguard. He would have heard the firing and would have ridden up, and would probably by now be close to your platoon. It should, however, be made clear that unless the platoon is actually replaced, it must carry on.

# SAND TABLE MODEL No. 4

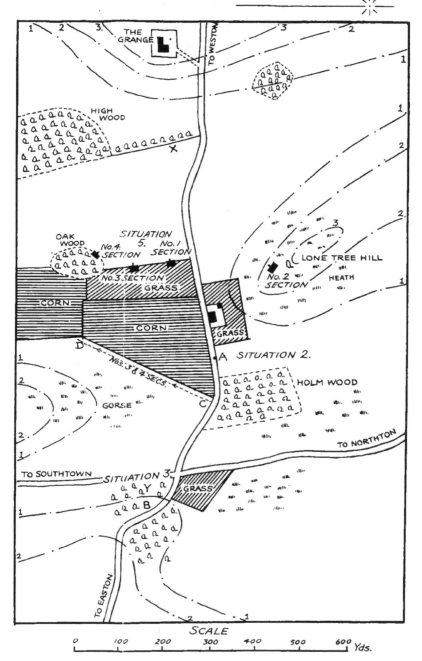

THE GRANGE

TO WESTON

HIGH WOOD

X

OAK WOOD

SITUATION 5.

No. 4. SECTION

No. 1 SECTION

No. 3 SECTION

GRASS

CORN

CORN

LONE TREE HILL

No. 2 SECTION

HEATH

GRASS

D

Nos. 3 & 4 SECS.

A SITUATION 2.

C

GORSE

HOLM WOOD

TO NORTHTON

TO SOUTHTOWN

SITUATION 3.

Y

GRASS

B

TO EASTON

SCALE

0    100    200    300    400    500    600 Yds.

# SAND TABLE EXERCISE No. 5.

## THE PLATOON AND SECTION IN THE OCCUPATION OF A DEFENSIVE POSITION

(Model used : Sand Table No. 5)

### 1. Object.

To study the action of platoon and section commanders in the organization of a defensive position.

### 2. Introductory.

Platoon and section commanders must realize that fire is the predominant factor in defence. However good a position may be and however protected by wire and other obstacles, it will be useless unless organized to produce a large volume of fire from all arms occupying it.

In " Infantry Training," Vol. II, Sec. 20, para. 10, we read—

" Every commander must organize his fire plan as thoroughly as the time, the conditions and the resources at his disposal will permit, so as to use his artillery, machine-gun, anti-tank, rifle, and light automatic fire in co-operation to the best advantage. **The Artillery fire plan, the siting of the infantry defence works, and the placing of wire obstacles, if available, must all be co-ordinated, as far as possible, to force the enemy into the arcs of fire of the machine guns.''**

In order to make the best use of this fire power, a defensive position is organized as follows :—

(1) The forward line of defended localities, held by platoons and sections. This is the line in front of which the commander has decided the attack must be stopped, and must be so sited as to give adequate protection to the positions which are required by the artillery for observation purposes.

(2) Defended localities held by companies and platoons, sited in relation to the artillery and machine gun fire plan, disposed in depth and affording each other mutual support by fire.

(3) Reserves so sited that they can use their weapons, and be prepared to counter-attack if necessary.

ORGANIZATION OF A DEFENSIVE POSITION.   DIAGRAMMATIC.

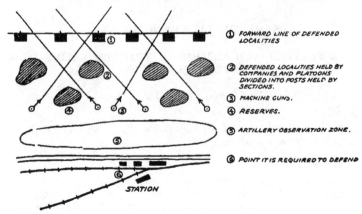

① *FORWARD LINE OF DEFENDED LOCALITIES*

② *DEFENDED LOCALITIES HELD BY COMPANIES AND PLATOONS DIVIDED INTO POSTS HELD BY SECTIONS.*

③ *MACHINE GUNS.*

④ *RESERVES.*

⑤ *ARTILLERY OBSERVATION ZONE.*

⑥ *POINT IT IS REQUIRED TO DEFEND*

STATION

## 3. Exercise No. 5.

A. NARRATIVE.

A force of all arms is taking up a position along the general line of high ground south of River EXE.

TOR FARM and EAST HILL are included in the forward line of defended localities.

B. PROBLEMS.

**(1) Situation 1.**—You are O.C. No. 1 Platoon, " A " Company, 1st Blankshires. You are allotted the area pointed out to you on the ground (marked on map) which has to be organized as a defended locality. You are responsible for the road MILLTOWN —OVERTON.

A section of machine gunners is getting into position to assist you in this task.

There are covering troops in front.

**Problem 1.**—How would you dispose your platoon in the area allotted to you ?

**Notes for Solution, Problem 1.**—The students should consider the action of the platoon commander from the time he receives his orders from his company commander. His platoon would probably be resting somewhere in rear.

He should proceed with the occupation of his locality in the following manner :—

    (a) Move his platoon up to a position just in rear of his locality where it will be covered from the air—*e.g.*, DEADWOOD PLANTATION.

27

(b) Get into touch with the platoon commander of the machine gun platoon operating in his sector of defence, in order that he can arrange to bring fire on those points not covered by the machine-gun fire, and also to ensure that he does not dispose any of his sections where they would mask the machine-gun fire.

(c) Go round his area and decide on the dispositions of his sections, bearing in mind the following points :—

(i) Section posts must give mutual support.

(ii) He must arrange mutual support with the platoon localities on each flank.

(iii) He must make the best use of natural cover, such as hedges, folds in the ground.

(iv) He must arrange for blocking the road and for the erection of obstacles.

(d) The platoon might be disposed as follows :—

No. 1 Section (Rifle) in hedge at B, in order to bring fire on the hedges and fields to the front.

No. 2 Section (L.G.) in TOR FARM to bring fire on slopes down to the river and north-west of GORSE HILL which is dead ground to No. 3 Section.

No. 3 Section (Rifle) in the open on the spur at D, to bring fire on the slopes to the front, and can bring fire on POST BRIDGE if required.

No. 4 Section (L.G.) in position at C. To block the road and bring fire to bear on the block. Also to bring fire in front of TOR FARM.

(2) **Situation 2.**—It is now 1400 hours. The troops which are covering the position are remaining out until 1900 hours. During this period the position is to be organized for defence. Three picks and three shovels will be available for each section.

You are O.C. No. 2 Section which has been ordered to take up position at A.

**Problem 2.**—Describe in detail how you would organize your section post for defence.

The detail for any constructive work you may decide to do is not required in this problem.

**Notes for Solution, Problem 2.**—(a) A section post should be organized for defence in the following manner :—

(i) Move section to concealed position if possible, in vicinity of section post.

(ii) Post sentry.

(iii) Decide on the exact position of the post, remembering that natural cover, if available, is always the best.

C 2

(iv) Decide on the type of construction to be done in order that each man can use his weapon.

(v) Detail men to tasks and arrange alarm post. Equipment may be taken off if there is a covering party in front.

(b) Whilst his section are busy on the construction of the post, the section commander will have time to choose reference points and make a range card as follows :—

(i) SUITABLE REFERENCE POINTS.—BRAY FARM, range 400 yards ; call that FARM.   HUNTER'S COPSE, range 300 yards, take near corner ; call that COPSE.

(ii) RANGE CARD.—All students should make out a range card similar to the following :—

## RANGE CARD

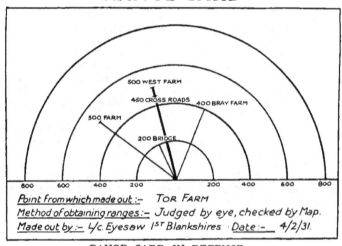

Point from which made out :—  TOR FARM
Method of obtaining ranges :—  Judged by eye, checked by Map.
Made out by :—  L/c. Eyesaw 1ST Blankshires · Date :—  4/2/31.

RANGE CARD IN DEFENCE.

(c) Having done this, he should practice the alarm and explain the reference points and range card to his section.

The method of giving orders to a sentry will form the subject of a later problem.

(3) **Situation 3.**—You are O.C. No. 1 Section, which has been ordered to take up position behind the hedge at *B*.

**Problem 3.**—What steps would you take to put this hedge in a state of defence ?

**Notes for Solution, Problem 3.**—With a little construction, a hedge can be made into an excellent fire position.  Care must be taken that any freshly dug earth is concealed, and that the enemy's side of the hedge should be left undisturbed in order that the position may not be given away.

The following diagrams show two methods of putting a hedge in a state of defence :—

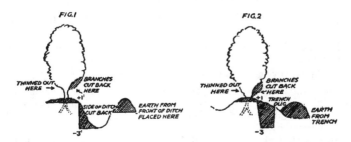

(4) **Situation No. 4.**—You are O.C. No. 4 Section, which has been ordered to take up a position at *C*, covering the road and blocking it.

**Problem No. 4.**—(*a*) What construction work would you do on this post ?

(*b*) Where and how would you block the road ?

**Notes for Solution, Problem 4.**—(*a*) The chief points to look for in the construction of the post are—

(i) Good fire position for the gun, with alternative positions on either side of the road.

(ii) Position which will enable the gun and rifles of the section to keep the road block under fire.

(*b*) It is suggested that the hedge should be cut through in order that there may be alternative positions for the gun—*i.e.*, so that it can cover the road and, if necessary, be moved to fire across the fields on either side (see diagram).

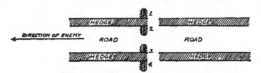

**Notes for Solution, Problem 4.**—(*b*) A good position for this road block would be at the point marked *X* on the map. It is just south of the bend in the road, so is under observation from No. 4

Section's post, but would be unseen by any mechanized vehicles until they rounded the bend.

If there are any trees in the vicinity, they could be felled across the road. If not, farm implements and carts could be brought from TOR FARM. These should be wired or tied together so that they cannot easily be pulled away.

**(5) Situation 5.**—You are O.C. No. 3 Section. You have been ordered to take up a position in the open at *D*.

**Problem 5.**—(*a*) What construction work would you do on this post ?

(*b*) What orders would you give the sentry on your post ?

**Notes for Solution, Problem 5.**—(*a*) This entails a digging of a post in the open, the first essential being that each man has a fire position. These positions can be joined up to form a small section post capable of all-round defence.

Slits are first dug 6 ft. by 3 ft. by 3 ft. These are then connected to form various types of posts, as shown in the following diagrams.

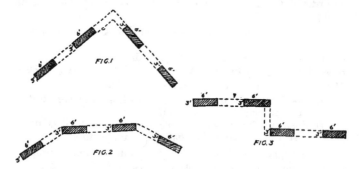

**Notes for Solution, Problem 5.**—(*b*) Section commanders are rather apt to learn off lists of points on which a sentry should be given orders, and then forget some of the essential points when he has actually to issue his orders. The following method is easy to remember and prevents any important points from being omitted :—

First give orders about everything to sentry's front—*e.g.*, what is known of the enemy, are there covering troops out, where roads lead to, reference points, names, etc.

Then going round in a clockwise direction, give orders on all points on the sentry's right, rear and left, finally returning to the sentry himself and giving him orders on points such as wearing of equipment, gas alarm, air alarm, challenging, etc.

Suggested orders are as follows :—

ORDERS TO SENTRY, No. 3 SECTION'S POST.

*Front.*  1. Enemy patrols were seen this morning in BLACK-TOWN, 10 miles north. There is no other information.

2. There are covering troops in front until 1900 hours.

3. Note these names. That river is the RIVER EXE. The bridge is POSTBRIDGE. That road leads to OVERTON, etc.

4. Reference points are POSTBRIDGE, 200 yards ; call that BRIDGE. STAG FARM, 400 yards ; call that FARM.

*Right.*  5. Sections on your right are disposed as follows. (Give positions of the other three sections.)

6. Note the names : That farm is TOR FARM, etc.

7. That road leads to MILLTOWN.

*Rear.*  8. Platoon H.Q. is with No. 4 Section. Company H.Q. is in DEADWOOD PLANTATION.

*Left.*  9. Point out places and positions of troops on the left.

*Post.*  10. This is your post. You will challenge any one approaching it and fire if they do not halt. Warn me if you see any hostile movement. Beat that shell case if you smell gas.

# SAND TABLE MODEL No. 5

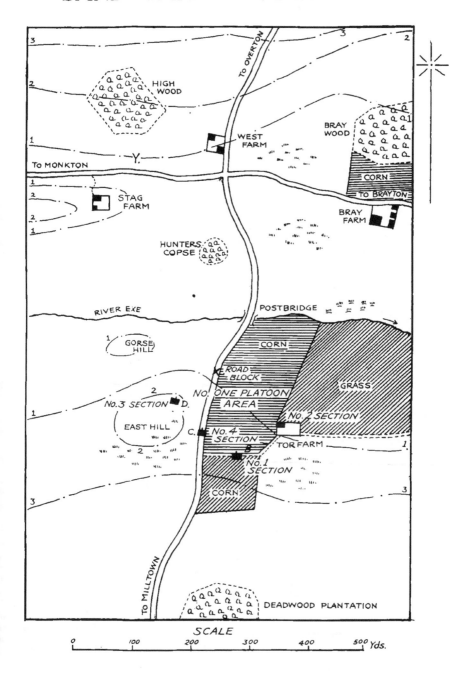

SAND TABLE EXERCISE No. 6

**THE PLATOON AND SECTION IN THE DEFENCE**

(Model used : Sand Table No. 5)

**1. Object of the Exercise.**

To study the actions of platoons and sections in the defensive battle.

**2. Introductory.**

It must be impressed on all members of platoons and sections occupying defended localities that it is just as important to surprise the enemy in defence as it is in any other form of operation. This can only be done by—

(a) Showing as little movement to the front as possible.

(b) Concealment of all construction work, such as covering up excavated earth, taking care not to break the natural line of hedges, etc.

Surprise **by** the enemy must also be guarded against, a constant watch must be kept on the whole of the front, and any movement observed must at once be reported.

It may often happen that the first information that a section commander may get of an impending attack will come from the rear, information having been received from the air that the enemy appear to be forming up for an attack. On the other hand, the sentry on a section post may be the first to see signs of an enemy attack by his own observation of the front.

It is most important that all information of this nature should be communicated at once to a higher formation.

**Do not fail to report something you have observed, because you think someone else has reported it.**

In peace training information is nearly always duplicated. In war this will not be so ; runners get killed, wires get cut, and whole sections may be wiped out.

In order to effect surprise the enemy may dispense with a preliminary bombardment, and the first intimation of an enemy attack may be the appearance of enemy sections advancing on your post, having approached under cover of darkness, fog, or natural cover.

**" All ranks must understand that once battle is joined, the troops allotted to the defence of a post or locality are responsible for holding it at all costs, and for inflicting the greatest possible loss**

33

**on the enemy. The fact that a neighbouring post or locality is captured must under no consideration be considered a reason for withdrawal."** (" Infantry Training," Vol. II, Sec. 19, para. 7.)

If the enemy penetrate the position, the battalion or company commander will organize a counter-attack, and great assistance can be given by fire to this counter-attack by any section or platoon localities which have not been overrun by the enemy.

### 3. Exercise No. 6.

#### A. NARRATIVE.

In continuation of the narrative of Exercise No. 5, the position has been occupied and the enemy covering party withdrawn. It is now 0900 hours. Reports from the air show that an enemy attack is likely to develop on the brigade front by midday. Six armoured cars were seen in OVERTON at about 0830 hours. This is about eight miles from your position.

#### B. PROBLEMS.

(1) **Situation 1.**—The sections are all in position as shown at the conclusion of the previous exercise.

You are O.C. No. 4 Section. Your platoon commander gives you the information contained in the above narrative.

**Problem 1.**—What would you do on receipt of this information ?

**Notes for Solution, Problem 1.**—(*a*) **As soon as you get information pass it on to someone else.** In this case tell all your section at once.

(*b*) Tell the sentry he must keep particular watch on the road OVERTON—MILLTOWN beyond WEST FARM for the approach of any armoured cars.

(*c*) See that you have plenty of ammunition and that all your magazines are filled and ready near the gun.

(*d*) See that each man thoroughly understands what he has to do in the event of an enemy attack.

(*e*) Impress on all men that there must be no firing without an order from you.

(2) **Situation 2.**—You are O.C. No. 4 Section. It is now 1000 hours. An enemy motor cyclist is observed proceeding along the road OVERTON—MILLTOWN coming from the direction of OVERTON. He stops at the cross roads and disappears behind a hedge. Shortly afterwards an armoured car comes along the same road and stops by WEST FARM. Two men get out and start looking at the engine. It appears to have broken down. A second armoured car appears and, seeing the first one halted by the side of the road, drives in behind WEST FARM. Two men

are seen to go to the assistance of the first car. Shortly afterwards two more armoured cars are observed approaching WEST FARM.

**Problem 2.**—What would you do ?

**Notes for Solution, Problem 2.**—(*a*) You have to decide at once whether you are going to fire or not. It is about 500 yards range, which is within the range of effective fire with the Lewis gun. What, however, would be the result ? A few casualties possibly amongst the personnel of the armoured cars, but little damage to the cars.

(*b*) This appears to be a case where the section commander should hold his fire, report what he has seen, and let the artillery deal with this target.

**(3) Situation 3.**—The last situation was dealt with by artillery fire. Three armoured cars were apparently put out of action, and one returned up the road in the direction of OVERTON.

At 1030 hours two enemy scouts are seen to come out of HIGH WOOD and cross the open space down to the hedge at Y.

**Problem 3.**—You are O.C. No. 3 Section. What would you do ?

**Notes for Solution, Problem 3.**—These men are probably the scouts of an enemy section. If you open fire on them, it will at once give warning to the section behind that they are shortly to come under enemy fire. If you let them come on, however, the enemy section will probably be drawn into the open and provide you with a good target.

It is suggested that this is a case when an anticipatory fire order might be given—*e.g.,*—

" No. 3 Section—500—Near end of HIGH WOOD—5 rounds rapid—Await my order to fire."

**(4) Situation 4.**—An enemy section appears and is engaged by No. 3 Section. There are two or three casualties, and the remainder gain the shelter of the hedge at Y. At 1040 hours an enemy section appears from BRAY WOOD and rushes across the road near BRAY FARM. Shortly afterwards light automatic fire is opened on No. 2 Section's post from one of the windows of BRAY FARM.

**Problem 4.**—You are O.C. No. 2 Section. What would you do ?

**Notes for Solution, Problem 4.**—You should engage the target at once. Suggested fire order is as follows :—

" No. 2 Section—400—BRAY FARM—Top left window—5 bursts—RAPID FIRE."

**(5) Situation 5.**—It is now 1100 hours. An attack in some force is developing on the whole of the front. Under cover of artillery fire, STAG FARM and HUNTER'S COPSE have been occupied by the enemy. An enemy section appears out of HUNTER'S COPSE, but at that moment your view is obscured by smoke shell which has been put down in your locality. As the smoke clears you see the section approaching POST BRIDGE.

**Problem 5.**—You are O.C. No. 4 Section. What would you do ?

**Notes for Solution, Problem 5.**—A brief fire order is required here at once, in order to engage this section as they cross the bridge. A suitable fire order would be—

" No. 4 Section—200—POST BRIDGE—RAPID FIRE."

**(6) Situation 6.**—It is now 1115 hours. The attack has further developed, and GORSE HILL is now in the hands of the enemy. Heavy fire has developed on all section posts from this locality, and under cover of the fire more enemy sections are rushed across POST BRIDGE. A strong attack is developed on Nos. 1, 4 and 3 Sections' posts, which are overrun by the enemy.

**Problem 6.**—You are O.C. No. 2 Section. (*a*) What action would you take on seeing the remaining sections of your platoon overrun by the enemy ? (*b*) Would you be justified in retiring to the high ground behind to avoid being cut off yourself ?

**Notes for Solution, Problem 6.**—(*a*) You should do all you can by fire to assist the defence. You are now in a good position to bring enfilade fire on any enemy advancing up the line of the road.

(*b*) You would not be justified in retiring. You must hang on to your position at all costs, and when a counter-attack develops you can be of great assistance if you still have retained your position.

# SAND TABLE EXERCISE No. 7

## THE PLATOON AND SECTION IN A WITHDRAWAL

(Model used : Sand Table No. 6)

### 1. Object of the Exercise.

The object of this exercise is to study the action of platoon and section commanders in a withdrawal.

### 2. Introductory.

Occasions arise when a commander is forced by the tactical or strategical situation to withdraw. In order to cover this withdrawal, a portion of the force is detached and called the rearguard.

The action of the rearguard should be studied under the following two headings :—

(*a*) When pursuit is not close.
(*b*) When in close contact with the enemy.

(A) WHEN PURSUIT IS NOT CLOSE.

A proportion of the force is detailed as a rearguard. This will depend on the closeness of the pursuit and how long it is required to delay the enemy.

" When the hostile pursuit is not close, the chief responsibility for delaying the enemy will devolve on aircraft, mobile troops, and the artillery. Offensive action from the air, long-range artillery fire, and demolitions all exercise a great delaying power on a pursuing force." (" Infantry Training," Vol. II, Sec., 32, para. 5.)

**Formation.**—The formation of a rearguard of this nature is best explained to platoon and section commanders by comparison with the formation of an advance guard.

A rearguard is divided into :—

(*a*) **Rearguard Mounted Troops,** which correspond to the advance guard mounted troops.
(*b*) **Rear Party,** which corresponds with the vanguard.
(*c*) **Main Guard,** which corresponds to the main guard of the advance guard.

The formation adopted is very similar to that of the advance guard shown in Exercise No. 4, only proceeding in the opposite direction.

37

The main duties of these divisions of the rearguard are as follows :—

(a) *Rearguard Mounted Troops.*—To endeavour to delay the enemy until the rear party has taken up a suitable position, and then to protect the flanks.

(b) *Rear Party.*—To occupy suitable positions from which to delay the enemy and to cover the withdrawal of the main guard.

(c) *Main Guard.*—The main guard will normally move along a road in column of route. It may be necessary, if the enemy press, to take up position with the whole of the rearguard.

(B) When in Close Touch with the Enemy.

(1) A rearguard as described in the previous paragraph may develop into a rearguard in close contact, or it may be that the forces are already in contact, and the commander has been forced to retire by some development in the situation. **It may often happen that this is impossible in daylight, and the commander will have to wait for darkness to cover his withdrawal.**

(2) The front is divided into sectors, and each sector has its own rear party. Rear parties are normally platoons under the command of an officer. **Withdrawal on the whole front must be co-ordinated, and this can only be done by a carefully timed programme.**

In orders for a withdrawal the following times are normally given.

(a) Time to commence withdrawal. At this time the battalion commander sends back his reserve company and some machine guns to the next position in rear, together with reconnaissance parties from all the other units in the battalion.

(b) Time thinning out may commence in forward companies.

(c) Time up to which forward positions are to be denied the enemy. At this time the rear parties leave the positions

(d) Time at which the rear parties are to cross a given line in rear.

(3) **No unit must withdraw without having a definite place to go to.** To ensure this the commander of each unit allots an assembly area in rear of his position where he can collect his sub-units. This is best shown by this diagram.

**Notes on Diagram.**—(1) No. 2 Platoon is rear party and acts as a fighting patrol on the company front.

(2) Nos. 1, 3 and 4 Platoons each withdraw a section at a time to assembly areas of their own and proceed to the company assembly area.

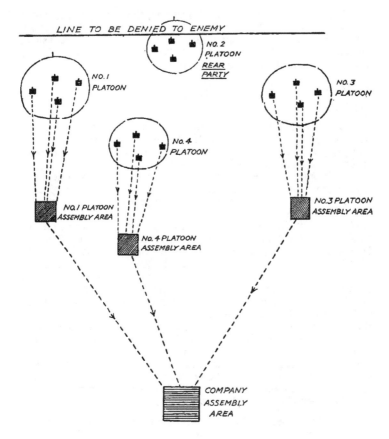

(3) At the time given up to which the position is to be denied to the enemy, the rear party leaves the forward line.

(4) The rear party crosses the co-ordinating line at the time given.

(4) A rearguard should afford the following :—

    (a) A close watch on all lines of approach.
    (b) Concealment.
    (c) Long-range fire.
    (d) Be easy to withdraw from.
    (e) Include all anti-tank obstacles available.

**" So far as infantry units are concerned, the principles governing the occupation of the localities allotted to them will conform generally to those laid down for defence. An extensive use of machine guns will lend strength to the position."** (" Infantry Training," Vol. II, Sec., 32, para. 10.)

## 5. Exercise No. 7.

(A) NARRATIVE.

The 2nd Bn. Blankshire Regiment is part of a force holding a position on the general line of the RIVER BROOK. " A " Company is the left forward company, and is disposed to cover crossing the BROOK south of PORTON.

" A " Company's dispositions are shown on the sand table.

At 0900 hours the company commander sends for his platoon commanders to come to company headquarters with an N.C.O. from each platoon.

He says : " The enemy do not appear to be advancing on our front, but have had some success on the right of our Brigade. It has been decided to withdraw to the high ground just north of LONTON. (Off the sand table.) A reconnaissance party will proceed to the rear position at 0915 hours. It will consist of my second-in-command, one N.C.O. from Company Headquarters and one N.C.O. from each platoon. This party will report to Battalion Headquarters and will then proceed to the rear position and be shown the company area by the second-in-command of the Battalion, who has already proceeded to the rear with O.C. Machine Gun Company. On reconnoitring the position, the party will rendezvous at Point (give map reference), where I shall meet it with the company. The N.C.Os. will then join the platoons and lead them to their new positions.

" The **method of the withdrawal** will be as follows :—

(a) 1000 hours. Withdrawal commences. No. 4 Platoon proceeds to rear position.

(b) 1030 hours. Thinning out may commence.

(c) 1100 hours. Position will be denied to the enemy until this hour.

(d) 1120 hours. Rear parties will cross the line of the road BROWNHILL—WESTON. (Off sand table to the south.)

" No 1 Platoon will be rear party.

" Company assembly area will be LONG WOOD.

" Withdrawal will be covered by No. 4 Platoon, ' D ' (M.G.) Company in position on our right, where he has a good field of fire, across our front."

He turns to O.C. No. 1 Platoon and says :—

" The bridge has been prepared for demolition and will be blown by Lieut. Wire of the R.E.   O.C. No. 1 Platoon is to give the actual order to Lieut. Wire when to blow it.   Lieut. Wire has also been given written orders to blow the bridge in any case should the enemy succeed in reaching within 500 yards of it before O.C. No. 1 Platoon can give the order."   (This is to ensure that the bridge does not fall intact into the enemy's hands.)

B. PROBLEM.

(1) **Situation 1.**—You are O.C. No. 2 Platoon (in position shown on sand table).   You have heard your company commander's orders and returned to your platoon.

**Problem 1.**—(a) How would you carry out these instructions ?

(b) What orders would you issue to your section commanders ?

**Notes for Solution, Problem 1.**—(a) (i) Decide on your order of withdrawal, bearing in mind that even though you have the cover of machine guns and of No. 1 Platoon, you must also cover your own withdrawal within the platoon.

(ii) Choose assembly area.   It is best to choose some feature that is easily recognizable on the ground to everyone.

(iii) If you have time, reconnoitre the best route to your company assembly area.

(b) Issue orders to your section commanders on the following lines :—

| | |
|---|---|
| *Information.* | The enemy are not pressing on our front at present, but have had some success on the right of our Brigade. |
| *Intention.* | To withdraw to the LONG WOOD area preparatory to taking up another position. |
| *Method.* | Platoon assembly area DALE WOOD. Withdraw in this order, starting at 1030 hours.   No. 5, No. 6, No. 7, followed by No. 8, which will be rear section, at 1050 hours.   No. 1 Platoon is rear party.   The withdrawal is being covered by a platoon of machine guns in position on our right. Choose your own lines of withdrawal to the platoon assembly area with a view to concealing any movement from enemy observation. |
| *Inter-Communication.* | Platoon headquarters will move with No. 6 Section.   Company headquarters is at LONG WOOD. |

NOTE.—Students should then consider the line of withdrawal of each section of the platoon and the formation to be adopted.

D

**(2) Situation 2.**—The withdrawal is carried out by your platoon in accordance with your instructions and you yourself move back to the platoon assembly area.

**Problem 2.**—In what formation do you visualize the platoon at the assembly area ?

**Notes for Solution, Problem 2.**—It is most important that sections do not bunch together in assembly areas. They may be in one of the open formations with intervals of at least 50 yards between sections. Until the platoon leaves the assembly area, No. 8 Section should be in position in the NORTH of the wood, watching the rear.

**(3) Situation 3.**—You are O.C. No. 1 Platoon which has been detailed as rear party.

**Problem 3.**—Describe briefly what your duties are as O.C. Rear Party in this case.

**Notes for Solution, Problem 3.**—(a) To co-operate with the Machine Gun Platoon commander and to cover the withdrawal of the company. The main avenue of approach through the position is the road PORTON—LONTON. My chief task is therefore to watch this road and prevent any enemy movement along it into the position.

(b) To keep the company commander informed of any enemy movement which may effect the withdrawal.

(c) Give orders for the demolition of the bridge.

(d) To keep the enemy off the position until 1100 hours.

(e) To withdraw in such a formation which will prevent there being any risk of surprise by the enemy.

**Problem 4.**—How would you carry out these duties ?

**Notes for Solution, Problem 4.**—(a) Get into touch with the commander of the M.G. Platoon. He can assist you by bringing fire down on the river crossing and beyond, but he will be useless if you should dispose any of your sections so as to mask his fire.

(b) Get into touch with the R.E. officer to whom you have to give the order for demolition.

(c) Give your orders for withdrawal and arrange a signal with the O.C. M.G. Platoon to let him know when you are moving.

(d) Issue orders on the following lines :—

| | |
|---|---|
| *Information.* | As in Company Commander's orders. |
| *Intention.* | To cover withdrawal of the company to the high ground north of LONTON. |
| *Method.* | The platoon will act as a fighting patrol. Platoon assembly area LONG WOOD. Nos. 1 and 2 Sections will commence withdrawing at 1055 hours. Nos. 3 and 4 |

Sections cover their movement with fire if necessary. At 1100 hours Nos. 3 and 4 withdraw to assembly area. If enemy are still not pressing the patrol will then proceed along the Road PORTON—LONTON with intervals of 50 yards between sections. No. 3 Section will be rear section. If enemy are pressing, the patrol will move back by bounds, two sections at a time covered by the fire of the remaining two, to positions which I will indicate.

The patrol will cross the line of the road BROWNHILL—WESTON at 1120 hours.

*Inter-Communication.*     Platoon headquarters will move with No. 2 Section. We shall meet our guide for rear position at (show on map).

NOTE.—Students should consider the action of each section of the patrol.

**Problem 5.**—You are O.C. No. 1 Platoon. Your company commander stated in his orders that the bridge was to be blown by your order to Lieut. Wire. Why did not he himself order Lieut. Wire to blow the bridge, and why did he say that Lieut. Wire had orders in any case to do so if the enemy reached a certain point.

**Notes for Solution, Problem 5.**—An order for the demolition of a bridge must always be given by the infantry officer on the spot. You are in touch with the local situation. If there are any infantry or cavalry patrols on the north side of the river you would be acquainted of this. " The rearguard commander may, in the case of a very important bridge, himself give the actual order for its destruction, **more often he will delegate the responsibility to some other officer.** (" Infantry Training," Vol. II, Sec. 32, para. 17.)

Cases have occurred in war where bridges have been prepared for demolition but have not been blown because no one gave the order. To avoid this happening, Lieut. Wire must be given orders so that he can blow the bridge should the enemy succeed in approaching it.

" The officer or N.C.O. in charge of the demolition will also be given written instructions that he is to effect the demolition himself should the enemy reach a certain position. **This will ensure that the demolition is carried out, should the officer detailed to give the order fail to do so.**" (" Infantry Training," Vol. II, Sec. 32, para. 17.)

D 2

**Problem 6.**—The withdrawal to the company assembly area is carried out without incident. In what formation do you visualize the company to be in when moving back from the company assembly area to the next position. Contact with the enemy has been broken.

**Notes for Solution, Problem 6.**—With intervals between platoons, and No. 1 Platoon acting as rearguard with one section as rear party.

# SAND TABLE MODEL No. 6

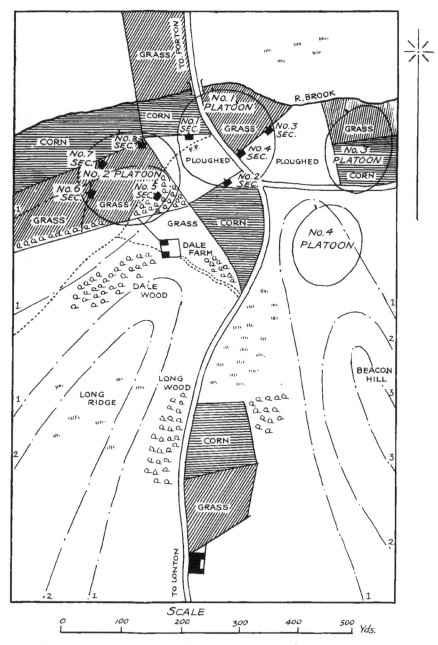

*Note:—* Only Nos. 1 and 2 Platoons are shown in detail.

# SAND TABLE EXERCISE No. 8.

## THE PLATOON AND SECTION ON OUTPOST

(Model used : Sand Table No. 7)

### 1. Object of the Exercise.

To study the actions of platoons and sections on outpost duty.

### 2. Introductory.

(1) DUTIES.

    (a) To ensure rest.
    (b) Prevent enemy obtaining information.
    (c) In event of attack, give warning to the main party to take up position.

(2) Principals same as for defence. Frontages wide, so depth may be sacrificed.

(3) ORGANIZATION.

    *Piquets.* One or more platoons corresponding to the foremost line of defended localities.
    *Supports.* One or more platoons. Primary action support by fire.
    *Reserves.* Give further depth and counter-attack if necessary.

(4) PROCEDURE IN TAKING UP A POSITION.

    (a) *The Outpost Company.*
      (i) Company moved to area of concealment in rear of position.
      (ii) Temporary alarm post.
      (iii) Covering party.
      (iv) Company Commander reconnoitres and decides number of piquets. Concealment important.
      (v) As soon as in position, covering troops withdraw.

    (b) *The Platoon on Piquet.*
      (i) Move to rear of area.
      (ii) Examine ground and decide on sentry groups. (Sentry groups to be never less than one section in strength.)
      (iii) Give orders.

45

(iv) Ensure that all men know—
> The direction of the enemy ;
> Position of various piquets ;
> What to do in case of alarm ;
> What the ground looks like by day, in case they have to go out at night.

**3. Exercise No. 8.**

A. NARRATIVE.

A Southland Brigade is advancing on WHITMORE and LONGMOOR. Its advanced guard has met with some resistance on the high ground in the vicinity of WESTHAM.

After a sharp encounter, the enemy have withdrawn in some disorder over the crossings of the River WYE in a northerly direction.

Owing to the situation in rear, the Southland Brigade commander is ordered not to cross the line of the River WYE until further orders.

He orders 2nd Bn. Blankshire Regiment to take up an outpost position just south of the River WYE.

B. PROBLEMS.

(1) **Situation 1.**—It is now 0900 hours. There are no further signs of enemy activity. Cavalry patrols report that there are now no enemy within five miles of the River WYE.

" A " Company is sent across to the north bank of the River WYE to form a covering party. The C.O. sends for company commanders to meet him on the high ground by HUNTLEY HALL.

**Problem 1.**—You are O.C. " C " Company. You are at present with your company about a quarter of a mile south of WESTHAM on the road CARDON—WESTHAM. You get a message telling you to meet the C.O. at the place ordered. What instructions would you give your second-in-command before leaving.

**Notes for Solution, Problem 1.**—Tell your second-in-command to move the company up into BOX WOOD and conceal them from the air. Your platoon commanders to come forward to the northwest corner of the wood and await you there. This will save you considerable time later on.

(2) **Situation 2.**—The area allotted to your company is the area covered by the sand table. " A " Company is on your right, and " B " Company is in reserve. A platoon of machine guns will be prepared to bring fire on the approaches to the river crossings.

The bridges will not be demolished, as they will be required by our own troops later on.

**Problem 2.**—How would you dispose your company in the area allotted to you ?

**Notes for Solution, Problem 2.**—The main considerations affecting the dispositions of the company are the river crossings, which are likely lines of approach by the enemy.

Suggested dispositions of the company would be as follows :—

(a) No. 9 Platoon to form No. 1 Piquet in PARTRIDGE COPSE, to watch the approaches from the Ford.

(b) Nos. 10 and 11 Platoons to form No. 2 Piquet at WESTHAM. A two-platoon piquet owing to the two important roads converging from the river crossings on to WESTHAM.

(c) No. 3 Platoon to be in support at HUNTLEY HALL.

Note.—Outposts are organized into piquets, supports and reserves. This does not mean, however, that all three have necessarily to be found by the same company.

In this case the company are finding piquets and supports, but the reserve is being provided by the battalion—*i.e.*, " A " Company, the reserve company.

(3) **Situation 3.**—The company commander takes the platoon commanders up and allots them their areas.

**Problem 3.**—You are O.C. No. 9 Platoon. What would be your first action on receipt of your orders ?

**Notes for Solution, Problem 3.**—Move your platoon into PARTRIDGE COPSE, concealed from the air, whilst you are making your reconnaissance.

**Problem 4.**—How many sentry groups would you require—

(a) By day ;
(b) By night.

Where would you place them ?

**Notes for Solution, Problem 4.**—(a) The ground on the right is open and can be observed from the piquet position. There is, however, some dead ground in front of OAK WOOD, and it would be advisable to place a sentry group at the forward edge of the wood to keep this area under observation.

The sentry over the piquet would be sufficient to watch the ground on the right.

(b) By **night** the sentry group at OAK WOOD should be given orders to withdraw if there are any signs of enemy movement. Care must be taken so that he does not withdraw on to your piquet and mask your fire.

All sentries would be doubled and bayonets fixed.

**Problem 5.**—Describe how you would occupy the piquet position.

**Notes for Solution, Problem 5.**—(*a*) Post sentry over piquet position, making sure he knows which areas to watch.

(*b*) Explain the situation to your section commanders.

(*c*) Point out position of the other piquets.

(*d*) Decide and point out alarm positions. Supposing that No. 1 Section had been sent to OAK WOOD as sentry group, the remaining three sections might be disposed as follows :—

No. 2 Section to take up position in hedge of cornfield.
No. 3 Section on east side of PARTRIDGE COPSE.
No. 4 Section in north corner of PARTRIDGE COPSE.
(These positions are marked on the map.)

(*e*) Arrange gas alarm, remembering that a whistle must not be used for this.

(*f*) Ensure that each man studies the ground in front.

(*g*) Assemble piquet in wood and practice alarm.

(*h*) Arrange for a latrine.

(*i*) If wire is available, wire your position. Even a trip wire is an obstacle at night and will possibly prevent you being surprised.

**Problem 6.**—You are O.C. No. 1 Section, detailed as sentry group at OAK WOOD. What orders would you give to your sentry ?

**Notes for Solution, Problem 6.**—Your orders to your sentry should contain the following points :—

(*a*) Enemy have retired in a northerly direction, and there are now no signs of them within five miles of the river.

(*b*) " A " Company are out in front as a covering party, but will be withdrawn as soon as the OUTPOST line is occupied. Don't mistake them for the enemy.

(*c*) The piquet position is in rear, in PARTRIDGE COPSE. No. 10 and 11 Platoons are in WESTHAM and form No. 2 piquet. You must watch that track and all the approaches to the river you can see.

(*d*) The password will be LONDON.

(*e*) Give names of all prominent objects.

(*f*) Report any signs of enemy movement.

(*g*) If anyone approaches your post, challenge. If he does not halt, fire.

(5) **Situation 5.**—You are still O.C. No. 1 Section, in charge of the sentry group at OAK WOOD. The covering party has been withdrawn.

At 1600 hours you see one enemy rifleman walking down the track to the Ford.

You can see no one else.

The sentry challenges him and he halts. You bring him into your post, and on questioning him, he says : " I ran away during the action yesterday, and I knew that if I went back I should be shot. I have therefore deserted."

**Problem 7.**—What would you do ?

**Notes for Solution, Problem 7.**—It is not the section commander's duty to question prisoners, but to send him back with as little delay as possible. In this case he should be sent back under escort to the platoon commander.

(6) **Situation 6.**—This situation deals with the action of No. 2 piquet.

**Problem 8.**—You are O.C. No. 2 Piquet. How many sentry groups would you require—

    (a) By day ;
    (b) By night.

Where would you place them ?

**Notes for Solution, Problem 8.**—There are two important lines of approach through your piquet position. The crossing from LONGMOOR is visible from the piquet position, and can be kept under observation by the sentry over the piquet.

The crossing from WHITMOOR, however, is not under observation. **By day,** therefore, it would be advisable to have a sentry group at LOW COPSE to observe the approach to the crossing.

**By night** it would be advisable to place another sentry group forward near the LONGMOOR CROSSING to report signs of any movement.

You know that a platoon of machine guns is prepared to bring fire down on the river crossings and approaches to them. You should get into touch with the machine gun commander nearest to you and make arrangements so that you can inform him at once of enemy movement reported by your sentry group.

Both these groups should withdraw on the piquet position if there are any signs of an enemy advance, taking care not to mask your fire or the fire of the machine guns.

NOTE.—Further problems could be given on this exercise on—

(1) The occupation of No. 2 Piquet position, the same procedure being adopted as in Problem (5).
(2) The occupation of the support position.
(3) The action of a reconnoitring patrol sent out from a support platoon. See Exercise No. 3.

NOTE.—It will be noted that the terms " piquet," " supports " and " reserves " have disappeared from the new " Infantry Training," Vol. II. The term " Protective Detachment " is now used. The old terms still exist in section leading, so have been left in this book.

# SAND TABLE MODEL No. 7

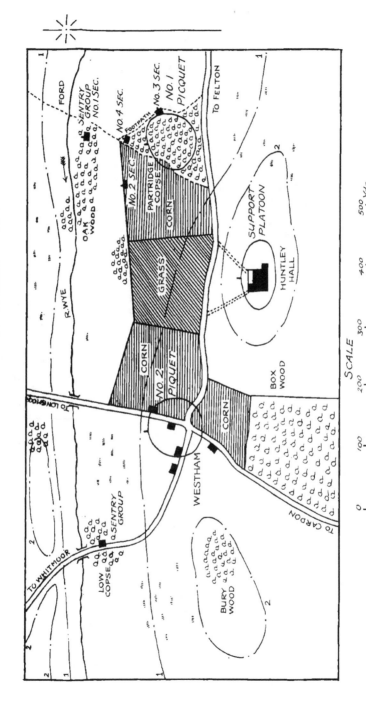

SAND TABLE EXERCISE No. 9.

## FIGHTING IN CLOSE COUNTRY—ATTACK

(Model used : Sand Table No. 8)

### 1. Object of the Exercise.

To study the action of platoon and section commanders in advancing through and attacking in close country.

### 2. Introductory.

(1) **" Any tract of country in which view and movement are seriously restricted by woods, hedges, etc., is termed ' Close country.' "** (" Infantry Training," Vol. II, Sec. 35, para. 1.)

(2) Close country restricts movement and makes control and co-operation extremely difficult. The season of the year, particularly in tropical countries, influences the tactics employed. Country which appears very close with little visibility during the rainy season, becomes open and easy to advance through towards the end of the dry season when the grass has been burnt.

Roads and tracks become of increasing importance. In very thick country it is often impossible to deploy from tracks without having to cut through the undergrowth. This restricts to a great extent the power of manœuvre.

(3) Infantry reconnaissance must be more detailed, as little information is available from other sources.

(4) **The Attack in Close Country.**—The same principles and tactical considerations as in any other attacks, but difficulty will be found in—

(a) Keeping control by the commander.
(b) Keeping touch between units.
(c) Overcoming the difficulties of the ground.

(a) CONTROL BY THE COMMANDER.—This can be done by—

(i) Selecting closer objectives than in open warfare.
(ii) Selecting objectives which **can easily be recognized on the ground** (such as roads, tracks, streams, etc.), and along which touch can be re-established.
(iii) Moving on a narrow front.
(iv) Keeping reserves well up.
(v) Using compass bearings.

51

(*b*) TOUCH BETWEEN UNITS.—This can be done by—

   (i) Co-ordination of troops on parallel tracks.

  (ii) Advancing slowly but steadily from objective to objective and establishing touch along each objective in order to check the direction of the advance.

 (iii) Carefully prepared methods of communication. Visual signalling generally impossible. Signal and smoke grenades. Wireless important. Runners used to a great extent.

(*c*) OVERCOMING DIFFICULTIES OF THE GROUND.—This can be done by—

   (i) Making as much use as possible of tracks and paths.

  (ii) Detailed reconnaissance.

 (iii) Facilitating movement of wheeled vehicles by finding gaps in hedges, etc.

 (iv) Remembering that the danger of losing direction is greatest when using covered approaches, crossing obstacles oblique to the line of advance, seeking gaps in obstacles and when fired on from an oblique direction.

(5) **Method of using compass for Flank Attacks in very Close Country.**—In very close country such as is found in tropical countries, troops are always sensitive about their flanks, and a carefully prepared and resolutely led flank attack often meets with success.

The chief difficulties are—

  (*a*) To locate the flanks.

  (*b*) Having located them, to so direct the attacking troops that the attack from the flank can be brought in at the right time and place.

The following method was practised in East Africa during the war with success :—

The enemy's flank having been located by careful patrols, the commander of the unit detailed to attack would be given orders which would contain the following :—

" Move 2,000 yards on a bearing of 45 degrees. You should then be 500 yards from the enemy's left flank At 1000 hours attack on a bearing of 315 degrees."

A telephone wire, if available is run out with the flanking party, who can then report when they are in position, and the commander of the force is then able to order the attack when he is ready. The attack both frontally and from the flank can then be co-ordinated.

ENEMY POSITION

ASSEMBLY POINT FOR ATTACK

500⁺ 315°

2000 YDS. BEARING OF 45°

LEADING COMPANY

REMAINDER OF COLUMN

(6) **Some Notes on Bush Warfare.**—(*a*) Transport will generally be by carrier, and even with great economy there will often be as many carriers as troops in a column. Carriers are quite undisciplined and liable to panic.

(*b*) A column commander will generally give instructions, flankers to be used throughout the force. They should be out as far as half the visibility as a general rule. That is to say, if the visibility is 100 yards, the flankers should be 50 yards from the column.

(*c*) Silence is of great importance, and shouting should be eliminated.

The following whistle signals in general use throughout the Royal West African Frontier Force are of interest :—

| | |
|---|---|
| Advance ... ... ... | 1 short blast. |
| Halt ... ... ... | 2 short blasts. |
| Out scouts and flankers ... | 3 short blasts. |
| In scouts and flankers ... | 4 short blasts. |

(*d*) In West Africa it is considered that Europeans are entirely unsuited to moving through dense bush, and are a hindrance rather than a help except in special circumstances. Senior N.C.Os. (native) are specially trained to run the scouts and flankers.

(*e*) It has been found from experience that in bush warfare it is seldom possible to fire the Lewis gun from the normal mounting, as the view of the firer is obstructed by the undergrowth as soon as he gets down behind the gun. Men of Lewis gun sections must therefore be trained to mount the gun in forks of trees and over branches, etc., about the height that a man can fire standing. This is the only way in which any field of fire can be obtained except along tracks.

(These notes are contained in " Notes on Training in Bush Warfare," issued by the Royal West African Frontier Force.)

**Exercise No. 9.**

The sand table represents very close country, mostly forest with occasional clearings.

A. NARRATIVE.

The 1st Battalion Blankshire Regiment is a detached force advancing in a northernly direction in pursuit of a native chief who has been giving considerable trouble.

All transport is by carrier as the country is situated in a tsetse belt, which makes it unsuitable for horses. No motor transport can be used.

B. PROBLEMS.

(1) **Situation 1.**—" A " Company, with one platoon M.G., are advanced guard to the force, with No. 1 Platoon as vanguard.

A friendly native reports that last night (July 14/15) parties of the enemy were known to be in MOMBA.

**Problem 1.**—You are O.C. No. 1 Platoon. You are ordered to advance on a bearing of 20 degrees (True).

(a) Convert this bearing to Magnetic.

(b) Set your compass to march on this bearing.

**Notes for Solution, Problem 1.**—(a) Give the class an imaginary variation for this locality ; then, if variation is West, add to True bearing to get Magnetic. If the variation is East, deduct the variation.

(b) Turn the glass cover until the small indicator on the outside of the box points to the required bearing. It will be found that graduations are marked round the outside of the box.

Clamp the cover at this bearing, and then turn the compass until the arrow comes directly under the luminous direction mark on the cover.

If you now keep the arrow under the luminous direction mark, it will be found that the hair line on the outer cover is pointing in the required direction.

(2) **Situation 2.**—At 0800 hours the leading section of the platoon has reached point A (marked on the sand table) without encountering any enemy.

**Problem 2.**—In what formation do you visualize the remaining sections of the platoon ?

**Notes for Solution, Problem 2.**—A platoon acting as vanguard moving across very open country on a compass bearing would probably move in diamond formation, but in close country this is out of the question. Better touch is kept and less noise made if the platoon moves in file with intervals between sections, and flankers on either side working at a distance of about half the visibility. If the leading section have to force their way through any obstacles, they make a path for the sections coming behind.

Suggested intervals are shown in the following diagram.

(3) **Situation 3.**—At 0805 hours the section commander of No. 1 Section, who has started to advance scross the clearing north of point A, reports that he has seen some movement in the trees on the other side of the clearing.

**Problem 3.**—You are O.C. No. 1 Platoon. What would you do on receiving this report ?

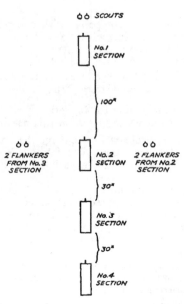

**Notes for Solution, Problem 3.**—(*a*) The platoon commander must bear in mind that he must not delay the advance of the force in rear. He has not time, therefore, to make a detour to avoid crossing the open ground in front. Nos. 2 and 3 Sections are close at hand, however, and he could quickly get them up to the edge of the clearing, where they can cover the advance of No. 1 Section across the open ground.

(*b*) Students should move their sections to the points where they consider they could best cover the advance of No. 1 Section.

**(4) Situation 4.**—The advance across the clearing is continued without incident. At 0815 hours No. 1 Section has reached point *B*, and reports : " I am unable to proceed further in this direction. I have come to a marsh which is impassable." This was unexpected. Lake GOMA was marked on your map, but no marshy ground shown to the west of it.

**Problem 4.**—You are O.C. No. 1 Platoon. What would you do ?

**Notes for Solution, Problem 4.**—(*a*) A detour must be made round this obstacle.

(*b*) Consider which direction. Lake GOMA is marked on your map, so the east is out of the question. You must therefore make your way round to the west side of the marsh.

(c) Instruct No. 1 Section to reconnoitre route.

(d) Note some prominent tree or object on the far side which is in the direct line of your advance, according to your compass bearing (Point C).

(e) Take your platoon along route of No. 1 Section round to the far side of the marsh to the prominent object you have noted, and continue your advance.

(f) Report this to your company commander. The O.C. Force can then avoid this obstacle, and will probably arrange to check the direction of the march on reaching the River VOLTA.

**(5) Situation 5.**—The advance is continued, and on reaching point D No. 1 Section is heavily fired on from the river bank in front by bows and arrows and muzzle-loading rifles. The Section is unable to advance beyond this point.

**Problem 5.**—You are O.C. No. 1 Platoon. From your observation from point D the enemy appear to be lining the river bank between the two tracks to your front.

(a) What action would you take?

(b) Write down any verbal orders which you would give to your section commanders.

**Notes for Solution, No. 5.**—(a) You decide to attack this position at once. Inform your company commander.

(b) Issue verbal orders as follows :—

| | |
|---|---|
| 1. *Information.* | |
| (a) *Enemy.* | The enemy are holding the banks of the river. Point out extent of their position. |
| (b) *Own Troops.* | No. 1 Section has reached point D, but is unable to proceed further. |
| 2. *Intention.* | I intend to attack this position. |
| 3. *Method.* | No. 3 Section to move up to edge of clearing on left of point D. |
| | No. 2 Section to move about 200 yards out to the left and find position to bring fire on to the river bank. |
| | No. 4 Section to move about 300 yards to right and find similar position. |
| | As soon as L.G. Sections are in position, open rapid fire on enemy position. |
| | I shall be with Nos. 1 and 3 Sections, and will advance on enemy under cover of this fire and assault the position. |
| | No. 2 Section will be able to continue firing longer than No. 4 Section. |

E

As soon as the advance of No. 1 Section masks fire of No. 4 Section, the latter will advance to river bank.

**(6) Situation 6.**—The attack is successful and the enemy retreat across the fords at $X$ and $Y$, and appear to take up a position in the trees in front of MOMBA. Any movement towards the ford bridge brings heavy fire from the new enemy position.

You have had very few casualties in the last engagement.

**Problem 6.**—As O.C. No. 1 Platoon, how would you deal with this situation ?

**Notes for Solution, Problem 6.**—(a) There are two crossing points—*i.e.*, $X$ and $Y$.

(b) Any crossing must be covered by the maximum fire you can produce.

(c) Suggested that the crossing be effected in the following manner :—

Nos. 1, 3 and 4 Sections develop heavy fire on enemy position whilst No. 2 Section crosses at $X$ and gets into a fire position on the opposite bank. As soon as No. 2 Section is in position and can fire, No. 3 Section can cross at $X$, covered by fire in a similar manner. No. 4 Section can then cross at $Y$ and get into position on the far bank. Finally, No. 1 Section can also cross at $Y$.

(d) Students should discuss the positions taken up by each section on crossing the river. Nos. 2 and 4 Sections, who are the first to cross at $X$ and $Y$ respectively, should not take up positions directly in front of the fords, or any fire directed at them will also hit the other Sections when they cross. The first Section over each ford should move out to a flank.

**(7) Situation 7.**—Under heavy fire produced by your platoon at such short range, the enemy suffer heavy casualties and retire in disorder. The enemy chief is found dead from a bullet wound in the head.

# SAND TABLE MODEL No. 8

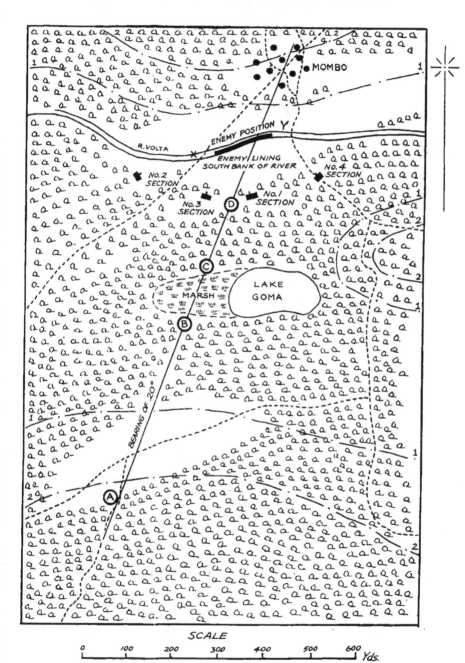

MOMBO

ENEMY POSITION Y

R.VOLTA

ENEMY LINING
SOUTH BANK OF RIVER

No.2
SECTION

No.4
SECTION

No.3
SECTION

No.1
SECTION

Ⓓ

Ⓒ

LAKE
GOMA

MARSH

Ⓑ

BEARING OF 20°

Ⓐ

SCALE

| 0 | 100 | 200 | 300 | 400 | 500 | 600 |

Yds.

## SAND TABLE EXERCISE No. 10.

### THE HORIZONTAL CLOCK CODE

(Any Sand Table Model may be used)

**1. Object of the Exercise.**

To practise the description of targets by the Horizontal Clock Code.

**2. Introductory.**

All officers and N.C.Os. should be familiar with the horizontal clock method of indicating targets to the artillery. They should also be quite clear in their minds as to what the artillery commander wants to know when a target is described to him.

Briefly, he wants to know—

(a) Where the target is, and where it can be seen from ?

(b) What type of target it is—*i.e.,* a machine-gun post, some enemy in a house, etc.—so that he can determine the type of shell he will use.

(c) When it was observed ?

In fire control orders when the clock face is used, 12 o'clock always points directly above the reference point, as observed from the section commander's position. In the horizontal clock code, however, 12 o'clock is taken to be approximately True North

NORTH

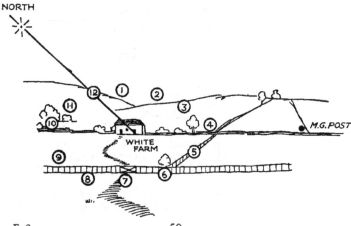

from the reference point. The advantage of this method is that the receiver of the message need not know the sender's position.

A reference point is taken as in fire control orders, but it must be some object which is marked on the map. If possible, it is better to have a reference point which has been agreed on previously with the artillery commander.

We will suppose that an enemy machine-gun post has been observed firing from a corner of a field South-East of WHITE FARM. This should be described in the following manner, the imaginary clock being placed with its centre over WHITE FARM and 12 o'clock pointing north :—

(1) Message sent back as follows :—
" Reference ALDERSHOT MAP, Sheet 303. WHITE FARM, 4 o'clock 900 yards, machine-gun post in hedgerow in corner of field. Can be observed from HUNTER'S COPSE X2904. 1159 hours."

(2) As soon as the battery starts firing, the imaginary clock is moved from the reference point so that its centre now coincides with the target and 12 o'clock pointing North.

(3) Each round is then reported with reference to the clock face and the estimated distance from the target given in yards—e.g., 6 o'clock 300 yards, 12 o'clock 150 yards, etc.

**Exercise No. 10.**

(1) Use any sand table model. Have a clock face cut out of cardboard with the numbers marked on it. See Diagram 2.

(2) Select a reference point and get a student to set the clock on a reference point. This should be done with reference to the actual True North point, so that if necessary a compass may be used.

(3) Point out a target and tell the class why you want to bring artillery fire on it—e.g., machine-gun post, party of infantry in house, etc.

(4) All students to write out a message reporting it to the artillery.

(5) Discuss the messages and criticize.

(6) Get one of the students to move the clock face so that its centre now coincides with the target.

(7) Place small pieces of cotton-wool on the sand table to represent the spots where the shells fall, and get the class to give their corrections for the artillery. In all cases this should be written down.

(8) Any number of targets can be taken in the same manner.

# APPENDIX.

Twenty Questions, with Answers, suitable for asking at Examinations on Section Leading Courses, and at N.C.Os.' Promotion Examinations.

*Question* 1.—What are the three different kinds of Fire Control Orders ?  Give an example of each.

*Answer* 1.—
    (*a*) Normal.
    (*b*) Brief.
    (*c*) Anticipatory.

(*a*) *A Normal Fire Order.*—" No. 3 Section—500—Quarter left, small clump of trees—6 o'clock, gap in hedge—5 rounds—Rapid fire."

(*b*) *A Brief Fire Order.*—" 200—Half left—Enemy advancing—Rapid fire."

(*c*) *An Anticipatory Fire Order.*—" No. 3 Section—500—Half-right, bend in road—5 rounds—Await my order to fire."

*Question* 2.—Show by diagram how a platoon halted, would move when signalled to :—

    (*a*) Deploy.
    (*b*) Deploy to the left.
    (*c*) Deploy from the centre.

*Answer* 2.—

| (a) | (b) |
|-----|-----|
| DEPLOY. | DEPLOY TO LEFT |

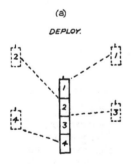 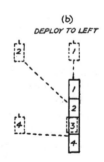

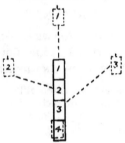

(c)

*DEPLOY FROM CENTRE*

*Question* 3.—On what frontages are the following generally employed in the attack ? :—
    (*a*) Battalion.
    (*b*) Company.
    (*c*) Platoon.

*Answer* 3.—

| | |
|---|---|
| (*a*) Battalion | 1,000 to 1,500 yards. |
| (*b*) Company | 400 to 600 yards. |
| (*c*) Platoon | 200 yards. |

*Question* 4.—What are the normal divisions of an advance guard ?

*Answer* 4.—
    (*a*) Advance Guard Mounted Troops.
    (*b*) Vanguard.
    (*c*) Mainguard.

*Question* 5.—The following force is detailed as a vanguard :—
    One Company of Infantry.
    One Platoon of Machine Guns.
    One Section of Light Artillery.

Show by diagram how you would expect this force disposed when advancing along a road before contact with the enemy has been obtained.

*Answer* 5.—See diagram, Exercise No. 4, Solution of Problem 1.

*Question* 6.—What are the duties of an advance guard ?

*Answer* 6.—(*a*) To reconnoitre, which may require offensive action to make the enemy disclose his strength and position.

(*b*) To brush aside the enemy's advanced detachments in order to prevent him obtaining information and to prevent the march of the enemy from being delayed.

(c) When opposition is encountered, which it cannot overcome, to seize and hold the ground necessary to the deployment of the main body.

(d) To pin the enemy to the ground and prevent him withdrawing.

*Question 7.*—What are the main duties of a section commander in the attack ?

*Answer 7.*—(a) To lead his section, choose line of advance, maintain direction and adopt most suitable formation.

(b) To co-operate with sections on his flanks and assist them with fire whenever he can.

(c) To choose fire positions, control and direct the fire of his section.

(d) To lead his section in the final assault.

(e) At all times to keep in touch with his platoon commander.

*Question 8.*—You are the N.C.O. in charge of a section in the attack. What action do you take on gaining your objective ?

*Answer 8.*—(a) Get into touch with your platoon commander and with neighbouring sections.

(b) Re-organize your section in readiness for a further advance.

(c) Be prepared to meet a possible counter-attack.

(d) Ascertain how much S.A.A. you have remaining.

*Question 9.*—What is the approximate area of ground occupied by the following in defence ? :—

      (a) Battalion.
      (b) Company.
      (c) Platoon.

*Answer 9.*—

| | | |
|---|---|---|
| (a) Battalion | ... | 1,000 yards square. |
| (b) Company | ... | 500 to 600 yards. |
| (c) Platoon | ... | 200 yards. |

*Question 10.*—As a forward platoon commander in a defended locality, what orders would you issue respecting the wearing of equipment, respirators, and lighting of fires ?

*Answer 10.*—Equipment to be worn except in case of working party when kept at hand.

Respirators always carried.

Lighting of fires forbidden.

*Question 11.*—What special points do you look to in organizing the defence of a platoon locality ?

*Answer 11.*—(a) Ensure posts are mutually supporting and sufficiently close to each other to enable him to exercise control, but not so concentrated as to constitute together a vulnerable fire for artillery.

(*b*) In conjunction with platoons on his right and left make such arrangements as are possible to ensure mutual support by fire as between localities, each covering ground which is dead to the other.

(*c*) So dispose his section that in the event of the platoon localities on his right and left being overrun by the enemy, his locality will be capable of all-round defence.

(*d*) Make the best use of natural cover available to obtain concealment and protection from fire.

(*e*) Take care that there is no dead ground in front where enemy can mass unseen. If this cannot be arranged patrol ground constantly.

(*f*) Strengthen defences as soon as possible by wire and improving natural cover.

(*g*) Ensure he has adequate supply of S.A.A.

*Question* 12.—You are a Lewis Gun Section Commander ordered to occupy a section post in defence. Describe in detail how you would proceed with the occupation of the post ?

*Answer* 12.—(*a*) Explain general situation.

(*b*) Detail men to tasks posting one as sentry.

(*c*) Select alarm posts.

(*d*) Decide how you will construct fire positions.

(*e*) See all magazines are full and ammunition adequate.

(*f*) Make out a range card.

(*g*) Select and indicate reference points.

(*h*) Practise alarm and gas alarm.

(*i*) Make arrangements for night.

*Question* 13.—What are the duties of outposts ?

*Answer* 13.—(*a*) To ensure rest for the remainder of the force.

(*b*) To prevent the enemy from gaining information.

(*c*) In the event of an attack to give the main body time to take up a position.

*Question* 14.—In order that an outpost can be occupied rapidly and methodically, what system is generally adopted in disposing the outpost troops ?

*Answer* 14.—Outposts are organized into :—

      (*a*) *Piquets*, consisting of one or more platoons and sometimes a whole company.

      (*b*) *Supports*, consisting of one or more platoons or a whole company.

      (*c*) *Reserves*, so located as to give further depth to the position.

*Question* 15.—You have occupied the section post and made all arrangements for the day ; what additional night arrangements do you make ?

*Answer* 15.—(*a*) Make out time-table of reliefs for his sentry post.

(*b*) Make cut-and-dried plan so that every man knows what to do in case of alarm.

(*c*) Look for and indicate to the men any means, such as object which would be silhouetted against the sky, which would serve as a guide at night to neighbouring posts and headquarters.

(*d*) Fix bayonets.

(*e*) Study ground with a view to going out on patrol.

(*f*) Make arrangements for night firing.

*Question* 16.—What are the different kinds of patrols which may be found in infantry in defence and outposts, and what would normally be the strength of each ?

*Answer* 16.—(*a*) Reconnoitring patrols ; strength, one complete section.

(*b*) Fighting patrols ; strength, one complete platoon.

(*c*) Standing patrols ; strength, one or more sections.

*Question* 17.—In what manner does the action of a reconnoitring patrol differ from that of a fighting patrol ?

*Answer* 17.—Both are sent out for *information*, but a reconnoitring patrol must avoid contact with the enemy. On the other hand, a fighting patrol is set a definite task and must be prepared to fight for its information if opposed by small parties of the enemy.

*Question* 18.—As commander of a patrol, upon what points would you require instructions before going out. Your task is reconnaissance and the strength of the patrol is one section.

*Answer* 18.—(*a*) What is known of enemy dispositions.

(*b*) Points on which information is required.

(*c*) Approximate route to follow.

(*d*) How far he is to go.

(*e*) Times.

(*f*) Movement of other troops in neighbourhood.

(*g*) Password.

*Question* 19.—In what formation would you generally move a patrol ?—

(*a*) By day.

(*b*) By night.

*Answer* 19.—(*a*) If country is open move in arrowhead, if a section ; and diamond if a platoon.

If country is enclosed, split patrol into groups and advance by bounds.

(*b*) Similar formations, but not so wide as by day. One pair should be able to escape if the patrol is suddenly attacked by a superior force. The whole patrol should be capable of putting up all-round defence.

*Question* 20.—You are the commander of a platoon employed as the leading detachment of a vanguard. What would be your action on finding that part of the road over which you were advancing was contaminated with mustard gas ?

*Answer* 20.—(*a*) Adjust respirators.

(*b*) If possible, direct your platoon around the contaminated area, otherwise they will get mustard gas on their boots and vapour on their clothing.

(*c*) Post gas sentries at the point where the contamination starts and ends, to warn troops in rear who will be advancing over the area.

(*d*) Report the locality to your platoon commander.

(*e*) If you have to advance over it, get the men's boots washed as soon afterwards as possible. At the first opportunity the boots should be brushed thoroughly over with dry bleaching powder.

CPSIA information can be obtained
at www.ICGtesting.com
Printed in the USA
BVHW061942291221
625115BV00005B/222

9 781783 314904